WHODUNIT
MYSTERIES

WHODUNIT MYSTERIES

More than 50 perplexing puzzles for you to solve

Joel Jessup

This edition published in 2023 by Arcturus Publishing Limited
26/27 Bickels Yard, 151–153 Bermondsey Street,
London SE1 3HA

AD011192NT

Printed in the UK

Contents

Introduction

Some time before the concept of a superhero entered the popular imagination, there was already a figure who embodied both the pursuit of justice and the excitement of seeing incredible powers utilised in that mission: The sleuth!

The powers that the sleuth exercises are not flight or strength but deduction, insight, and an understanding of human nature. Sometimes they are young and strong, physically chasing around after leads and suspects. Sometimes they are seemingly innocuous and harmless and preferring to sit in a large chair with an innocent expression while they weave a web around their prey. What separates a sleuth from the ordinary detective is their ability to gather all the clues and solve the puzzle, finding the truth beneath the skin of deception.

They are a naturally reassuring figure, even when they are eccentric or flawed, and a story of even the most dastardly or dark crime seems bearable when there is a sleuth doggedly moving everything towards the light. Learning the solution is a form of catharsis and revelation as your own theories are either cleverly confirmed or surprisingly subverted.

Each of the stories in this book is a little puzzle, your chance to accompany the sleuth on their journey of discovery and, at the end, you get to try and deduce the identity of the culprit. All the clues and evidence you should need is present, though it may not always be easy to spot!

The Level One stories are simpler, with only a few details necessary to understand the truth, and the Level Two stories are slightly more complex with multiple elements. Hints are available for each story, but only if you want to use them.

Your investigations will be spearheaded by 4 sleuths:

Joe Hollobone is a seemingly harmless odd-job man whose thick glasses and short stature hides a criminal past and a sharp mind. He likes fixing things, whether it's houses, objects, or the unsolvable crime.

DI Radford and **DC Axton** are a pair of police investigators. Radford was a former professional footballer, who joined the force after a leg injury, rising to Detective Inspector due to a combination of determination and his own minor fame.

He has taken under his wing Wilfred Axton, an apparently wooly-headed young man who has a remarkable ability to spot things that no-one else can.

Mary Fitzgerald is a young female singer from a privileged background, whose time in London has led her to develop a love of jazz music. This bright young thing often finds her incredible insight into human nature called upon by her many friends and acquaintances.

Helen Parnacki, the niece of the famous detective 'Paddington' Parnacki, is to all appearances an unobtrusive, shy woman, and for some reason she often appears in a variety of different menial jobs just when some kind of mystery is afoot. Sometimes she even solves the crime without those present realising she did so.

Happy detecting!
Joel Jessup.

Level One
CASES

1. The Telltale Hands

"You need the lock fixed?" asked Joe Hollobone, hefting his bag of tools through the doorway and staring at the young man who stood inside the office.

"This is a crime scene, sir," said the young plainclothes constable.

"It's no problem, Robinson, I know Joe," said the inspector from inside. "The lock will need fixing at some point, it may as well be now."

Joe nodded in a friendly manner to Knatchbull, and began diligently examining the broken lock, evidently shattered by some impact if the splintered wood around it was any indication.

"This'll do for interviews, Robinson," Knatchbull remarked. "Keep Mr Dabbs and Mr Bates outside for now, we'll talk to Mrs Birtles first."

It seemed Mr Cedric Birtles, an expert on work efficiency and scientific management, had been murdered in his apartment, which was directly above his office, the one they currently occupied. His wife had called the police at 9:30pm. The medical examiner suggested his time of death was at around 5:30pm.

"You found him slumped over his desk?" Knatchbull asked a tearful Elsie Birtles, the victim's wife.

"Yes, he had that knife sticking directly in his back, it didn't look real," she sobbed, twisting a handkerchief in her hands. "I knew something was wrong when I saw the lock had been broken, same way as that one!"

She pointed at where Joe was.

"Did he usually work at home?" asked Knatchbull.

"Oh yes, I know his office was only here, but he always said that you must be ready to work at a moment's notice. We even had pens and paper in the bathroom!"

"And you say you had been staying overnight with your sister?"

"Oh yes, she's been very down since her Albert died, I got off the train at Chichester station at 9pm and came straight here."

Joe had finished repairing the lock, and had already managed to wind the late-running office clock and fix a wobbly table by the time Peter

Dabbs was brought in. Joe couldn't bear to see something not working properly.

Birtles' assistant was very precisely turned out, with a crisply ironed suit and slicked–down oily hair. He looked only mildly inconvenienced by Birtles' death.

"Yes, we usually keep a small amount of petty cash, some certificates of value, do you think that is what they were trying to take?" he asked the Inspector.

"That's what's missing, but if his apartment adjoins his office why did they need to break in twice?" The Inspector asked.

"They adjoin but do not connect."

"That doesn't seem very efficient," the Inspector said doubtfully. "He leaves his apartment, walks all the way round to the front of the office and comes in that way every day?"

"You see, that is what people misunderstand about scientific management!" said Dabbs stridently. "Mr Birtles' studies showed that it was actually more efficient to have them separate than connected. I live my work life according to his principles!"

"And you were in here when he was murdered?"

"If, as you say, he was killed at 5:30pm then yes, I was here. I have a very precise schedule, arriving at 8:30am every day, paperwork, cup of tea with a single biscuit at 11am, meetings until

3pm, and so forth, then at 6pm I leave and catch the number 34 bus home. It's all here on this timesheet. Mr Birtles would be on the desk next to me, starting half an hour earlier than me and finishing half an hour later, though of course I understand he would sometimes continue to work upstairs."

"And you heard nothing?"

"At 5:30pm? No, although Mr Birtles' house is very well insulated. No doubt after I left the murderer noted my absence and proceeded to break in and steal the valuables."

"And you didn't see anyone?"

"Like the tempestuous Mr Bates? No. In fact as you can see, I was out for lunch at 12pm and therefore cannot even verify if, as he says, they met at that time."

"He was a chancer!" spat Jack Bates after he had been led in, his burly frame barely fitting in the chair as he clenched and unclenched his hands.

"I hire him to make my butcher shop 'efficient' and he comes out with all these expensive ideas! I tell him I haven't got that kind of cash and he says he doesn't care, he wants paying anyway, so I told him where he could stick his advice and he says he's going to report me to health and safety, well I tell you I was livid!"

"Yes, passers-by do report hearing raised voices at about 12:30pm," said Knatchbull.

"Nah, it was one o'clock I think," said Bates, pointing at the clock on the wall.

"And where were you at 5:30pm, Bates?" asked Knatchbull.

"I was at the pub where your constable collared me, wasn't I?" Bates sneered.

"Well, you're the only person he was scheduled to meet today. But we'll look into whether anyone else was here."

"No need," said Joe Hollobone from the stool where he was fixing the lightbulb. "You've already interviewed the killer."

Who does Joe Hollobone suspect of killing Cedric Birtles, and why?

Hint: Clock

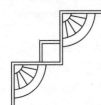

2. Instinctive Detective

Considering the precarious nature of her singing career since she decided to move into the field of jazz, Mary Fitzgerald was somewhat nervous to be currently ascending the elevator to the penthouse flat of theatrical impresario Victor Balanov. But the circumstances of her visit were so bizarre that she barely had time to acknowledge the butterflies in her stomach, let alone feel them.

Her companion on the journey up was Alicia Von Kessel, her long-time friend. Alicia was a more established singer and lyricist and, crucially, Balanov's former fiancée. And their visit was not a congenial one. Alicia had grabbed Mary by the elbow at a drinks reception the previous night and begun hissing in her ear about impersonation.

"I promise you Mary, the man who broke up with me was not Victor! The week before it was all normal, we'd finally managed to give away Ludwig's puppies. Then I was away all weekend and on Monday he broke off our engagement!"

"Did he explain why?"

"He wouldn't let me get close to him, claimed he had a wicked case of influenza and that he didn't want to infect me! Then he was blathering on with some rot about how his increased frailty made him feel unworthy of my hand and I suddenly started thinking how his skin looked rather odd, sort of waxy..."

"From the flu?"

"No, make-up, a wig, I swear it. Itt was an imposter!"

"Who?"

"It has to be Basil Krendler!"

"The man of a million mugs?" said Mary, quoting the poster of Krendler's most recent show.

"Who else? He's been pestering Victor for a part in his new revue. Krendler gambles like a fish drinks water, he owes money to all sorts of wrong'uns. I dread to think what he's done with my dear Victor! You must come with me tomorrow and confirm it!"

"Me? I've never met Mr Balanov or Krendler! Whatever use can I be?"

Alicia made a dismissive face. "Come now, you're sharp as a hat-pin."

And so here she was stepping out of the elevator and knocking on the penthouse door. A dour looking valet answered and with great reluctance led them into the drawing room where the man who could be Balanov sat at the opposite end from us behind a grand piano, swathed in scarves. He did not look pleased. Mary didn't think his skin looked particularly waxy, but then she hadn't seen Balanov's face outside of newspaper articles and concert programs.

"Alicia, I said it was better that we never saw each other again," he said in a strained, clipped accent with hints of Russian.

"Oh, Victor dear, I'm not trying to rekindle our arrangement, I simply wanted you to meet my friend Mary, I think she would be perfect for the role of Princess Vasilisa in The Firebird!"

Balanov made no attempt to stand so Mary gave him a small awkward wave.

"Um, hullo!" she said. "Are you still feeling poorly?"

"I think it is best you leave," he said coldly.

Alicia swung her bag round and accidentally knocked a plate of almonds onto the floor.

"Oops, silly me!" she pantomimed. "I'll go fetch Trumson to clear this up." Then she leaned over to Mary.

"Check out his face!" she hissed into her ear then theatrically exited the room. Suddenly from nowhere a tiny Pomeranian emerged and made a beeline for the spilled almonds.

"Ludwig, no!" Victor shouted. "He cannot eat them!" He dashed forward and managed to scoop them up before the dog ate any. Ludwig briefly growled at him then padded off. Victor suddenly realised he was standing next to Mary and nodded apologetically.

"I imagine she has told you I am an imposter?" he said casually.

"Um, it did come up," said Mary.

Ludwig shook his head slowly, sadly.

"She's telling everyone I wouldn't come close, that I had flu, the truth is I discovered that she has been unfaithful, our marriage is to be only one of convenience, for her bank account, at least! I tried to let her down nicely, but she spreads wild lies, and now she has roped you in. Look at my face!"

He leaned forward and tugged at his hair and moustache.

"Does this look like makeup? Does this hair look false? I can feel no hate, only pity, but you must both leave."

Alicia returned with the dour valet who peered unenthusiastically at the almonds in his master's hands.

"Well, we must be off!" said Mary brightly, steering Alicia towards the door.

"So, what do you think?" asked Alicia in the lift on the way down.

"I'm terribly sorry Alicia," said Mary. "But you are absolutely right. That's not Victor Balanov."

How does Mary know it's not Victor Balanov?

Hint: Dog

3. Indentation

Detective Inspector Radford regarded the statue with a dubious eye.

"It's Apollonia, you say?" he asked Detective Constable Axton, who, as usual, was walking around the room, his eyes wide as he absorbed information.

"Yes, the patron saint of dentistry! Maybe they thought it would keep people in the waiting room from worrying, you know, they're being overlooked."

"It's just a statue, Axton," said Radford.

"I suppose," he said, peering under its left arm. "No marks here..."

Radford shook his head slightly and walked into the office to interview Percival Winchester, the dentist in question.

The Surrey Police Force had received the call at about 9am that morning. Winchester's dental surgery had been broken into with considerable force and completely trashed, and expensive dental equipment had been stolen.

Radford was, however, feeling rather relaxed about this one because although there had been no witnesses there was a major piece of physical evidence: a bite mark on the arm of the statue!

"It's Arthur Sumpter!" hissed Winchester, as if afraid to speak the name. "About four months ago I saw him walking along the high street and his teeth were... incredible. I have never seen such a conglomeration of dental misfortunes in a single mouth! Decay, abnormal eruptions, excessive gingival display... I had to get an impression from him, so that I could show a plaster cast of them at the next association gathering. That is where the trouble began..."

"It was like a row of condemned houses!" said Rachel Talbot, Winchester's dental nurse, who had entered the room. "And his breath, phew! Once we got him the chair and began taking the impression of the top teeth, he started talking about how he was going to be famous, and how much money he was going to make...”

Winchester reddened at this. “Yes, it was rather inappropriate, and I fear I was too soft on him, we finished the first impression and rushed him out of there, giving him a bob for his trouble. But then he began coming to the surgery every day, asking if I’d heard anything, wanting to see my tools and talking about how much money dentists make. He was obsessed!”

“But you did show his teeth at the conference?” Radford asked, tapping the bronze cast of Sumpter’s top row on the table. Winchester seemed to be using them as a paperweight.

“Certainly, yes, but the money I gave him is more than 10 times that you would normally give a subject of study...”

“And you began asking the local constables if they could scare him off?” asked Radford, who had seen the reports.

“Only once he started getting threatening!” said Nurse Talbot. “He was getting angry that he hadn’t heard anything and started asking for more money, implying we were taking advantage of him! It was frightening!”

“I simply asked Constable Grenville if he would have a word,” said Winchester. “And it helped at first, we didn’t see Sumpter for almost a week, but then he began lurking, not speaking to us but simply staring with rage... And he was following Nurse Talbot home!”

“Is Enkins a common surname?” asked Constable Axton as he entered the room.

“...What?” asked Winchester with confusion.

“You have a chart for a Mr Enkins there,” he said, pointing at a white folder on the desk. Axton reached over and then rubbed white powder from its cover. “It’s Jenkins, it was just some dust covering the J...”

“Please forgive my constable, he’s... curious,”

said Radford, ushering Axton back into the waiting room. "So, you told Grenville about Sumpter's increasingly threatening attitude…"

"We did, but he said while he could keep warning Sumpter he couldn't lock him up unless he committed a crime!" said Winchester.

"Which he now has! I came in and found the place trashed, the statue's arm bitten! What if I'd been here, would he have bitten me too?" said Talbot with fear.

There was now the sound of a commotion in the waiting room and Radford slipped into it, closing the office door behind him, to see a man who was undoubtedly Sumpter being held in an arm lock by local Constable Grenville.

"Get off!" Sumpter yelled, and Radford could hear muffled cries of concern coming from the office behind him.

"Why have you brought him here, Grenville, and not the station?" asked Radford wearily.

"He's a right wiggly one sir, and since I knew you were here, I thought this made more sense."

"I ain't done nothing!" said Sumpter, glaring.

"These bitemarks say otherwise!" said Grenville, pointing at the statue's arm.

"Bite mark," corrected Axton, casually reading a copy of Punch that he'd found on the table.

"I ain't strong enough to bite a statue's arm!" said Sumpter, calming.

"Actually, the statue's made of plaster, it would be more than possible for someone to bite it," said Axton not looking up.

"I couldn't have done it; I was sick at home!" Sumpter said.

"Grenville, get him down the station…," said Radford.

"No, don't!" said Axton, closing the magazine. "He's innocent."

How does Detective Constable Axton know Sumpter is innocent?

Hint: Cast

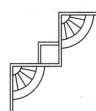

4. The Three Georges Paxman

Joe Hollobone entered the hospital and after a short conversation at the front desk was guided to Ward F by one of the nurses, meeting Inspector Knatchbull at the door.

"Alright Joe?" Knatchbull said, "We were hoping to sort this all out here, hope you're not too shaken by that body you found?"

"No, I'm alright," said Joe levelly, noting cracks in the plaster of the wall. "Not my first."

Joe had been asked to do some small repairs to a beach hut in West Wittering. While there he had noticed rats scurrying from the ramshackle hut next to it, and on investigation he had found an undressed body inside, that of a middle-aged man with short brown hair and a large beard, but otherwise no distinguishing features of any kind. The body had only underpants on and no other indication of clothing other than some tiny bits of blue fluff.

The rats had not done much so it can't have been there long and once he found a policeman the body was transported away.

"The hut belonged to a man named George Paxman, he roughly matches the description of the body but then so does every other blighter in this area," said Knatchbull, shaking his head. "Is it too much to ask for a hook or an eyepatch? Anyway, we don't think the body is him."

"Why not?"

"Well, to start with, we have this gentleman…"

Knatchbull led Joe into the ward where one of the beds was occupied by a scruffy, confused looking man in a hospital gown. His hair was short and brown, though shaggily cut. His skin was sun-baked, but for a whiter area around his mouth and chin that he kept rubbing thoughtfully.

"He was found wandering along the seafront this morning. His clothes were soaked but his wallet and ID say George Paxman, and we found some soggy pieces of paper in his pocket, certificates? It all chimes with our description of Mr Paxman as a banker. He even has a monogrammed shirt and a gold watch with the engraving 'to George, from Cecily'. Presumably a sweetheart."

"Presumably? Can't he say?" asked Joe.

"Well, that's the thing, this fella says he's lost his memory."

"The words George Paxman din't mean nothin to me," the bedridden man  said in a strong Scottish accent. "But if'n they say that's who I am then who am I to argue wi'that?"

"Do you remember anything, sir?" shouted Knatchbull, as if to a child.

"Naw, naw...It's all a blur, just wooden poles and sand and... darkness."

Knatchbull pulled Joe aside. "By all accounts Paxman wasn't Scottish. And I don't think a dip in the sea changes that, even if you have a goose-egg on the back of your head like our friend here. And then we have the third George Paxman..."

Knatchbull lead Joe through into the visitor's room where a nervous looking young man in navy argyle sweater and tightly pressed beige trousers was wringing his hands. He had a wispy brown beard and wild, unwaxed hair.

"Around about the time the gentleman in the bed was found staggering along the pavement this young man came into the police station and announced himself as George Paxman, said all his things had been stolen."

"I AM George Paxman!" said the young man after Knatchbull entered. "That man out there... well, it's quite embarrassing but I came down to Brighton for the weekend with a friend... a lady...We were going for a late-night dip, and I decided to... disrobe. I didn't want to ruin anything! Then when I came back my clothes and items were gone!

He must have taken them!"

"Will the lady confirm this?"

"No, she... wasn't supposed to be here. She got me some clothes and ran off. And you mustn't tell Cecily! But he has all my things, so he has to be the thief!"

"He has no memory of this, sir," said Knatchbull.

"You said he has no memory of anything!" said the man. "Presumably after robbing me, he drank a bottle of gin and bashed his head falling over!" he now looked at Joe who had begun adjusting the height of one of the lamps, wondering why he was there.

"And how do you explain the body in your beach hut, Mr 'Paxman'?" asked Knatchbull.

"I have no idea!" said the young man, turning pale. "I did say I'd lend the keys to my friend Alan, he's down here too waiting for his ship to sail, but without seeing the body I have no idea who it could be. I hope it's not him... perhaps that tramp out there attacked him too! Or maybe they were conspiring to impersonate me!"

"Well, this is quite a pickle," said Knatchbull as he led Joe out. "Three possible George Paxmans. One in the right place but dead and undressed, one with the clobber and personal items but no memory, and a third who says he's the real one but can't prove it. Whoever it is, he's in for a windfall, those soggy documents we found were shares in United Steel Companies."

A constable appeared and whispered to Knatchbull.

"Apparently they spoke to the bank where he works, and they said Paxman was a young man with short brown hair and clean-shaven," said Knatchbull. "But I don't see that helping us much."

Knatchbull peered back at the visitor's room.

"Still, once we get hold of a friend or relative, we'll sort it out."

"No need," said Joe. "I know who the real Paxman is. And you'll want to arrest him."

Who does Joe think is the real George Paxman, and why does he need to be arrested?

Hint: *Shaved*

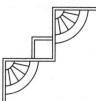

5. Deeper Freeze

If there was a competition for accurate operation of a typewriter while talking at a fast pace, the two ladies sitting in front of Helen Parnacki would get equal first place.

"I told you that cold storage room was a menace, no-one ever checks on a Friday! And that door swings shut like a steel trap!" said the first. "If you don't have the keys, that's it!"

"It's not a menace Ida, it's just a freezer. Where else will they store the cherries?" said the second.

"They say fresh on the packet, should be fresh in the pie! But that's not the point Betty, Enid Almond is!" said Ida, effortlessly.

"A frozen Almond amongst frozen cherries," said Betty..

"Betty!" said Ida.

"Sorry Ida," said Betty, smiling.

"What was she doing in there anyway?" continued Betty. "She never goes in there, that's worker's business. That's why she didn't have keys!"

"I heard..." said Ida, leaning in conspiratorially, "...that she was looking to have an assignation with that young man in packing, whatsisname, Gino Ginelli!"

"Francesco Guinotti!" corrected Betty, then blushed.

"Ooh Betty, you don't fancy him do you?"

"No! I'm just an eighth Italian, that's all..." she blustered. "Anyway, he's too young for her..."

"I don't disagree love, but there it is, I heard him confessing to the sergeant, all 'she said she'd meet me here at 8pm' and 'I came but she wasn't there!'"

"And she froze to death waiting for him? Blimey!" said Betty, fanning herself. "But if he knew she was in there, he should have said something!"

"No, apparently she said to meet in the office, no clue why she was in there. Unless..."

And then Ida pursed her lips very tightly as if to prevent the words from leaving her mouth.

"...It was murder..."

Betty's eyes opened very wide at this. "What, Francesco?"

"No... Mr Almond," Ida said in a very quiet voice.

"MISTER ALMOND?" shouted Betty, before reacting to Ida shushing her aggressively. "THE Mr Almond? You'll get the sack, talking that way."

"What, telling the truth?" said Ida, boldly. "We knew there was trouble in paradise, him saying she's spending too much on hats and shoes and what have you, her calling him stingy."

"Well, he is very frugal," said Betty. "These walls haven't seen a lick of paint in an age, and there's more woodworm in the broom handles than wood..."

"That's the thing Betty!" said Ida as if presenting a piece of evidence in court. "They found one of the brooms in the freezer, snapped in two just by the door they said! What if Mr Almond lured her in there and 'wallop!', then he drags her behind the cherries and it's off to Margate!"

"I, um, don't think that's likely," interjected Helen, timidly.

The two ladies turned to her, and Ida briefly considered admonishing her for eavesdropping, but in the end her desire for fresh information won out.

"Why do you think that love? It's Hettie, isn't it?"

"Helen. Parnacki."

"Like Paddington Parnacki?" said Betty.

"A bit like," replied Helen. Before Betty could ask more Ida butted in.

"What have you heard?"

"Um, well, I did happen to hear one of the constables say there were claw marks on the inside of the freezer, so I don't think she could have been unconscious when she, um, froze."

The two ladies reeled back as they processed this unpleasant detail.

"Well then, it was clearly murder wasn't it," said Ida. "I never knew Mr Almond had such a cruel streak!"

"Well..." continued Helen. "Mr Almond was here earlier, and he told the police Enid wanted to meet him here too. About 7:30pm. In the office as well. He says he came, and she wasn't here"

"And you just happened to hear that too?" said Ida, recognizing a fellow busybody.

"Oh, um, I happened to be passing by. With some files." said Helen.

"Well I never!" said Betty. "What a carry on."

"It's clearly a lie though," said Ida. "She'd never ask to meet both men so close together, one must be lying!"

"Well, he'll be making a fortune out of it," said Betty. "She's got quite a life insurance policy, they both do, I saw the files. Maybe he sees it as a way of getting all his money back."

"Maybe," said Helen, her eyes sharp. "Or maybe, the person who killed Enid Almond wasn't quite as clever as they thought."

Who does Helen Parnacki suspect killed Enid Almond?

Hint: Broom

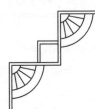

6. Debutante in the Dark

Mary liked many of the people at this Debutante ball, but the whole idea made her roll her eyes. When she'd been in line to attend her own several years previously, she'd faked an attack of gastroenteritis, very convincingly she thought. But at this event she was here in her capacity as an entertainer. Her uncle had agreed that she could perform 20 minutes of songs, provided she stuck to "popular songs and none of that jazz". She reasoned she'd gauge the crowd, and if enough of them got suitably merry on the wine and champagne on offer she'd slip in a bit of Cole Porter and see if anyone objected.

Looking around at the assembled young women, stuffy older people, and assorted minor royals, she decided most of them were either in their cups or so self-obsessed that you could sing sea shanties and they wouldn't notice.

Several of them had clustered around the famous perfumier Giles Fontaine. He had created a special fragrance for Felicity Grant-Naylor, one of the more elevated debutantes at the ball, and many of the other attendees hoped he might be convinced to do the same for them. Fontaine looked like he was under the impression it was a fancy dress ball as he was wearing a pirate costume with hat, puffy shoulders, and an eyepatch.

At the polar opposite of the social scale was Sir Gerald Ffolkes, a blustering sort with a red face. He was Felicity's fiancée and the kind of fellow who believed gunpowder was the only decent smell and who cared little for the French. Felicity herself was in an adjoining room with a small group of friends preparing for her big entrance.

Mary greeted a few of her friends in the crowd and overheard Fontaine complaining loudly.

"It is disgusting, the smell of these canapes!"

"Oh Giles dear, you do go on. The tray is practically on the other side of the room!" said an older lady by his elbow. In response Fontaine tapped his nose.

"Mon nez is as sensitive as your English bloodhounds. This room is a soup of cheap tinctures and corked wine."

Mary rolled her eyes and practically bumped into Ffolkes, who had been glowering at Fontaine.

"Steady on old girl, don't come barrelling out of nowhere!" he snapped.

Mary nodded an apology and headed to the dressing room to prepare for her performance, but it was not to be, because at that moment all the lights and power in the venue snapped off!

Fumbling her way into the main hall, all that could be seen was shadows, any ambient light blocked by the thick curtains on the windows. People were murmuring and shouting in confusion, and there was great relief when the lights snapped back on.

At this point Felicity grabbed Mary's elbow and swung her into the coat-check room, dismissing the girl inside with a wave of her hand.

"Oh Mary, you have to help me. I just know they're going to blame Grantham for this!"

"For what?"

"The jewel of Tanzania, someone just snatched it off my neck!"

"I had no idea you were wearing it!"

"No-one did! I may have told him about it, in confidence! I was so excited when Sir Gerald gave it to me. He insisted I save it until our wedding, but I managed to get him to agree I could wear it tonight if I hid it in a locket."

"I see, but who's Grantham?"

"Grantham Figg! He's a troubled young man I've been helping through Daddy's foundation. He's had a bad lot in life, and I wangled him a job as a waiter at this, trying to get him a step up. But once the police have had a look at his past, they'll be convinced he's the thief and it won't matter what anyone else says!"

"He's a thief?"

"Was, Mary, was! He's completely reformed!"

"And he didn't know about the necklace…"

Felicity blushed. "I may have mentioned it to him, out of excitement."

"Mary thought carefully. "Who else here knows about it?"

"No-one, I didn't even tell my maids! No, wait, I did mention it to that French perfume chappy, Fontaine. I'm wearing my new fragrance tonight and I wanted to make sure there wasn't anything in it that would react strangely with the necklace."

"Hmm. It could still have been a theft of opportunity; everyone knew you were getting ready in the dressing room and might have thought there were goodies to be taken…"

"That's just it though Mary, when the lights went out I was actually round the corner in a service corridor eating a profiterole! Mummy's got me on a beastly diet. So I don't know how the thief found me!"

Mary considered this. "Grantham would of course have access to the corridor."

"Oh but Mary, he's really reformed, honest! And whoever it was didn't feel like him, he's a twig! They had big shoulders."

"Like your fiancée?" said Mary, arching an eyebrow. "He's a famous hunter, isn't he, surely he could have tracked you in the dark?"

"Ffolksey?" Felicity gave a short laugh. "Sir Gerald is blind as a bat without his glasses, and he never wears them in public!"

At this point Felicity looked over Mary's shoulder and gave a yelp, and Mary turned to see a sallow spindly youth in a waiter's outfit being manhandled by a policeman. Mary turned back to her stricken friend.

"Don't worry Flick. I know who did it."

Who does Mary Fitzmaurice suspect stole the necklace?

Hint: *Scent*

7. Forbidden Fruit

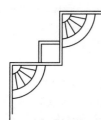

"Jolyon Tenscott's the name!" bellowed the broad-chested businessman, shaking Gordon Stokes' hand. "Just arrived in Blossomdale on the 3:20 train, very much looking forward to seeing the famous Stokes cherry orchard!"

Stokes's calloused palm left red stains on Tenscott's softer one. Tenscott stared at it with distaste.

"Cherry juice," Stokes muttered, and then stalked towards the cottage.

"Of course!" said Tenscott, beckoning the secretary girl to join him.

"Jolly hot out here!" he continued. "Woollen suit a bad choice I suspect. And my pomade seems to be manna to the local horseflies."

Stokes grunted. Inside the cottage was very spartan and sitting formally at the kitchen table was a weathered looking old woman and a boffinish young man with a great resemblance to Stokes.

"This is Ma and Malcolm." Stokes grunted.

"Ah, Phyllis Stokes, and your genius brother!" blurted Tenscott, sitting uninvited at the table. "Jolyon Tenscott's the name..."

"And you are, ma'am?" said Malcolm to Tenscott's secretary, who seemed to try and hide behind him.

"Oh, don't mind her, she's just a recorder. Padwacky or something," said Tenscott dismissively. "I'm sure you know why I'm here! After your father's unfortunate passing in the orchard the receivers at Almond's Cherry Pies want to ensure that there will be no interruption in the supply of its cherries, seeing as this farm supplies, um..."

He snapped his fingers at the girl, who shuffled a few papers.

"47 percent of all fruit contents for the pies!" she said meekly.

"That's it, 47 percent! They're depending on your supply, especially as you pre-stone all the cherries here before shipping them, and while mourning is all well and good, needs must etcetera, you do understand."

The mother burst into tears and Malcolm consoled her. Gordon Stokes stared balefully at Tenscott.

"The cherries'll come," he said. "Two pickers died of the pox last summer and the cherries kept coming. Fire blight took half the orchard in twenty-seven and the cherries kept coming. Wild wolves..."

"Oh give it a rest," snapped Malcolm. "We've all heard the saga."

"You've heard it, but you weren't here for it, were you, college boy?" snarled Gordon at his brother.

"I came back, didn't I?" said Malcolm. "I had to. But I don't think Mr Tenscott is interested in that..."

"Our concern..." interrupted Tenscott. "Is that Dennis Stokes was a figurehead in Blossomdale, and I worried that without him the ship might be a bit adrift..."

"A bloody tyrant, more like!" shouted Phyllis, then clasped her hands over her mouth and burst into tears again.

"Mother is a bit overwrought," said Malcolm, cleaning his glasses. "Mr Tenscott, you need not worry, my special breed of cherry trees is particularly tough and resistant to disease."

"Then why did the branch fall off onto your papa, if you don't mind my asking?" said Tenscott.

"Got to trim the trees sometimes," said Gordon. "Dead wood."

"I'm surprised it finished him off actually," replied Malcolm. "The old man was tougher than any of the trees in the orchard. Although that all-meat diet wasn't so helpful in his dotage."

"Well, um, I imagine it was actually the cyanide that killed him." Muttered the secretary.

All present turned to look at her, although the only one who looked surprised was Tenscott.

"Miss Padlock, what the blazes are you talking about?" he asked.

"It's Parnacki, sir, and the local doctor's report stated that he had a sufficient quantity of cyanide in his body to cause..."

"Where did you get the doctor's report?" said Tenscott, and the others in the kitchen also seemed curious about this.

"Oh, um, I arrived here yesterday sir, did a bit of preliminary research, if that's OK with you. The report had been, um, squirreled away a bit."

Tenscott perused the Stokes family, who looked suitably shifty. "Well?" he said.

"Arsenic is present in small quantities in all fruits with seeds and stones," said Malcolm knowledgeably. " The doctor's report clearly picked up on father's cherry consumption, so we felt allowing it to become public would give the wrong impression."

"Well, um, that would make sense, except that he wouldn't be eating the stones, would he?" said Helen Parnacki.

"But Constable Hardwick said there was no signs of foul play!" said Phyllis, looking stunned. "He checked around the village and no-one bought or sold any cyanide! And there were no outsiders here neither!"

"No-one comes to Blossomdale," muttered Gordon. "And nothing leaves but cherries."

"Well, it's a bit worrying..." said Tenscott, subdued by the strange turn of events. "We can't have people thinking there might be poison in Almond's Cherry Pies..."

"I think I can clear all this up," said Helen Parnacki. "The police will be here shortly, and the answer is simple."

Who does Helen Parnacki suspect of murdering Dennis Stokes?

Hint: Pits

8. No Ball

Detective Inspector Radford shook his head as he gazed over the cricket pitch at the prone body, hastily covered in cricket jumpers to preserve the dignity of the fallen batsman. Why did he always get the odd ones? Why not a good old-fashioned assault and battery?

"The ball exploded?" he said to Sgt. Billingsdale, the local policeman.

"I've never seen the like!" said Billingsdale, astonished. "Leather and willow everywhere!"

It was the 29th over of the morning session, fifth day of a five-day county match between Middlesex and Surrey here at Uxbridge Sports Club, and the crowd was sparse and disinterested as the match was grinding to an inevitable draw and the most interesting thing that had happened for hours was when a pigeon lazily wandered onto the pitch and fell asleep.

Sir Leonard Braxton-Spummer was at the crease, 18 runs not out having faced 173 balls already, when Tom Butcher bowled him a beamer which suddenly detonated two inches from his face! The crowd screamed as Sir Leonard collapsed to the ground.

"Jolly inconvenient," said a stoic Tom Butcher. "Was just about to break for lunch and that happens. Didn't really fancy scotch eggs after that."

"I assume you know this couldn't be an accident." Said Radford, noting down Butcher's lack of remorse at Braxton-Spummer's death.

"If you mean, do I know that cricket balls don't usually explode, yes I do," said Butcher. "But if you're accusing me then I must object."

"But crowd members reported that you did bowl it directly at his face...," said Radford.

"The weight was a bit off. Probably full of dynamite or something. I just bowl the balls I'm given."

"And who gives you them?" asked Radford.

"That'd be Grumpy McCogan, the umpire. He's the sour-faced old trout telling your young constable to stop ripping up the grass."

Radford turned and swore under his breath at the sight of DC Axton squatting down with a handful of grass while Mr McCogan red facedly berated him. Radford marched up and hoiked Axton up by his armpits while fixing McCogan with a stern look.

"What's this gormless boy playing at?" yelled McCogan, who then suddenly bit his tongue when he realised who he was addressing.

"I'm sure Detective Constable Axton has an excellent reason for... What were you doing Axton?" said Radford sharply.

"Sniffing pigeon droppings, sir," said Axton. "Something a bit odd about it."

"I should coco!" shouted McCogan.

"I mean the way they smelled. My dad keeps pigeons, their business doesn't smell like that. This was a bit chemical."

"Go wash your hands," said Radford, pushing Axton towards the clubhouse.

"You gave Butcher the ball that exploded?" Radford said before McCogan could continue ranting.

"I bear no responsibility for the condition of the balls!" said McCogan. "The club has been very lax on maintenance recently!"

"I don't think the ball exploded because it was in bad shape, Mr McCogan. Did you know the victim?"

"Everyone knew Braxton-Spummer, he was unavoidable. If you're looking for someone with a motive, half the club owed him money and the other half was owed by him. And the devil practically lived on the crease, I'm surprised he didn't set up a bivouac in front of the stumps."

"He rarely ran?"

"Yes, and he was difficult to get out too, Butcher can tell you about that, he's never bowled him once! Except this last time, in a way... If anyone had it in for him, it would be Murray–Hill, he was the other batsman but never got a chance to bat!"

Murray Hill was a beaming, ruddy-cheeked fellow enjoying a glass of port in the clubhouse.

"Oh no, never had any issue with old Spummy. I've a bit of a gammy leg anyway so it suits me not to have to run a lot."

"Why do you play, then?" asked Radford, noting that Axton seemed to be rummaging through the player's dirty kit in an adjoining room.

"The camaraderie! Though I think the quality of our opponents has gone down, like that Tom Butcher shower. Always walking around with his hands in his pockets, whistling. Always throwing bouncers as well."

"Bouncers?"

"You know, ricochet the ball off the pitch. Very effective."

Suddenly Axton thrust a small round metallic object in Radford's face.

"Look, sir, it's remarkable! This must have been the prototype."

"For the exploding ball?"

"That's right! Very short fuse. Then you put it inside a cricket ball shell. It would feel the exact same weight!"

"Did McCogan notice anything about the ball at the time? Or Butcher?" Radford asked Murray–Hill.

"No idea old chap, I think we were all looking at the pigeon."

Radford beckoned Axton over. "OK. I think we've caught our killer."

Who does DI Radford suspect of killing Sir Leonard Braxton–Spummer?

Hint: *Short Fuse*

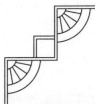

9. Manual for Murder

When Mary arrived at the police station, Gideon Grantham met her at the door before she went in. He looked exhausted and sad.

"Thanks for coming, Mary. I felt that you would be the best person to help calm Celia down."

"Is it true? She killed Tony?"

"That's what she said. When the police found his body in the crashed car they went straight to the mansion, and she confessed immediately! She had fiddled with the accelerator."

"But she doesn't know anything about cars!"

"She borrowed his manuals, worked it all out. She even showed them the grease under her nails! He must have gone out in it, lost control and ended up crashing. Somehow, he escaped any chest injuries from the steering column, but his neck snapped like...it's too awful to say."

Mary rubbed her forehead. "But Celia wouldn't, she's not a murderer!"

Gideon sighed. "I think she thought he'd just crash and get a nasty bruise and a scare. But you know what my dear bro was like, he drove that beastly machine like it was hell's chariot. Celia's not in her right mind, Mary. To be honest I feel like this whole Petunia business drove her to it, uh, pun not intended."

Petunia Crane was Tony Grantham's not so secret lover, a controversial female race driver. Celia's marriage to Tony had always been rocky but this latest dalliance seemed to be the last straw.

The police let Mary in to see Celia, who looked like she hadn't slept in days, wild bloodshot eyes darting around. "Oh Mary, I never thought... I just thought..."

Mary hugged her, but her mind had begun to turn things over.

"Celia, we need to think for a second. Are you certain it was your fiddling with the car that caused the crash?"

"But... but what else could it be? I banjaxed the accelerator and he went straight into a tree! The police said it was a complete fireball! All the petrol cans he had in there made it even worse!"

"So, you made it go fast... But why didn't he brake, did you mess with that too?"

Celia suddenly stopped crying, struck by this thought.

"No, but... I suppose he must have not had time! Or else he skidded into the tree!"

Mary turned to Gideon, who was hovering by the door.

"Can we speak to the detective in charge?"

Detective Inspector Bugg looked extremely weary at the thought of further analysis of this crime.

"Mr Grantham, your sister-in-law has confessed to your brother's murder. It's an open and shut case I'm afraid."

"Were there skid marks at the scene of the crime?" asked Mary. Bugg looked at Gideon with a sour expression, then at Mary.

"No, you see young lady..." Bugg said as if to a child, "it seems the victim had an injured foot, as he was seen in his driving outfit and goggles limping to the garage by a footman, 20 minutes earlier. No doubt he was unable to press on the brake with sufficient force."

"I saw Tony that morning and his foot was fine!" said Gideon.

"Asking your brother for money, according to the butler," said Bugg raising his eyebrow. "Please do not interfere in police business, Mr Grantham." Bugg said.

As Mary and Gideon left the station he swore in frustration. "Damn it all, I know nothing about cars! We need to speak to an expert!"

"Yes, I fear we do," said Mary thoughtfully. "But not for the reason you think."

They found Petunia Crane tinkering with a car in a subterranean garage. As they walked up, she gave them a sardonic wave and shuffled over to them with a wince.

"Oh hullo, here to pin the murder on me?" she said sarcastically.

"How can you be so insensitive??" Gideon shouted.

"Oh, I'm not allowed to have feelings, I'm only the mistress."

"We just wondered if you thought there was anything odd about the crash?" said Mary.

"So you can exonerate Little Miss Sabotage? It is a bit strange he didn't come to meet me. We were supposed to go on a little cocktail drive in my Alvis F-series, but he never showed. Maybe he was miffed that I always want to have the wheel. Typical boy stuff, like when he was annoyed, we were almost the same height. I assume he decided he'd rather drive his own car around instead."

"I'm just a bit uncertain how Celia messed with it," said Mary. "His car was an Alvis too, could you show me with your car?"

"It's being repaired," said Petunia sharply. "And you'll understand if I'm not much inclined to play teacher today. If you're looking for a different suspect, perhaps your friend Gideon here would suffice. You're the one inheriting everything, aren't you dear heart?"

Gideon looked apoplectic but Mary guided him out of the garage.

"Mary, I'd never harm Tony, I mean he was a terrible prig but..."

"Gideon, don't say anything else. It's time to go back to the police."

Who does Mary think is responsible for the death of Tony Grantham?

10. Into A Corner

Joe Hollobone sighed when he saw the floor of the dress shop. Three entire cans of paint had been knocked over and their contents poured all the way across the new carpets he had spent the previous two days fitting. What a waste.

The owner, Martin Belgeddes, had contracted Joe on the recommendation of other local businessmen. He was doing the fittings while a local painter named Arnold Cadogan gave the place a fresh coat. Joe didn't really know Arnold well, but his mother had a good reputation, and the lad was fairly diligent, if a bit late to arrive in the mornings.

Belgeddes had closed the shop during the renovation but still lived in a connecting flat and so was standing in front of Joe in his dressing gown looking mortified. But not only about the paint.

"I've been robbed!" he wailed. "I had 20 pounds in the till from Thursday and it's gone! I can barely afford this refit already, and now this happens!"

Joe looked at the slick of paint in front of him. One set of large boot prints could be seen in the spill, walking into the shop. Normally this would be a godsend to the police, as they could track down whoever owned the paint-covered boots, but the culprit apparently already thought of this as the boots in question had been removed and were on the floor in the middle of the room, just beyond the spill.

"Stay here, don't move," said Joe. "Police are still going to need to see the prints without you walking over them."

There was no alternative entrance or exit to the shop or even Belgeddes' flat, and the paint pool was too big for anyone to jump over or circumvent in any other way, so Belgeddes would have to remain there while Joe fetched the local constable.

Once Constable Mendip had taken note of the boot prints and got a colleague to photograph them (both for the police and for any insurance claim) the police felt it safe to enter and soon the paint was covered in many more boot-prints, both entering and leaving, causing Joe's eye to twitch slightly.

Arnold Cadogan arrived, late as usual, his eyes bugging out of his head.

"What happened?!" he gasped.

"Where were you last night!" shouted Belgeddes at Cadogan.

"Was I supposed to be painting last night? I was only doing days!"

"No, there's been a robbery my lad." Said Sergeant Mendip. "You are the only one who had a key to the premises apart from Mr Belgeddes and Mr Hollobone here."

"What? I never robbed the place. Why don't you think he did it?" said Cadogan, pointing uncharitably at Joe.

Joe could see that Mendip was weighing in his mind whether to say to Cadogan that they didn't suspect Joe because everyone locally knew he was a notorious former criminal and if he'd robbed the place, he wouldn't have made such a hash of it. But instead, Mendip decided to say

"That's a fair point sir, and he'll be helping with our enquiries, same as yourself. Can you tell us where you were last night?"

"I was having dinner with my Mum! She'll vouch for me! I'd never rob Mr Belgeddes, he's been very fair to me." He said, nodding to his employer. Belgeddes looked briefly mollified, then had a thought.

"Wait a minute officer, there is someone else who has a key! Sandra Cake! Why didn't I think of it before!"

Belgeddes explained how Miss Cake was his former shop assistant until he found out she'd been trying the dresses on without his permission. He'd sacked her but she'd never returned the key, and he had given up trying to pursue her for it when he'd decided to get the shop renovated and hire a new girl afterwards.

Miss Cake was located nearby and denied any involvement. "I forgot I even had his stupid key. All day in that shop with barely anyone coming in, and he fires me just for trying on dresses? Anyway, I've been working at the Odeon checking tickets. That's where I was last night, my bosses will confirm it."

"It would be fairly easy for you to slip out when the lights go down though," observed Mendip.

"Well, check my feet then!" she said. "Whoever did this had to fit those boots, didn't they? I'm definitely not a size 10."

"True, but you might've worn bigger boots to throw us off the scent!" said Mendip wagging his finger at the girl.

"It was probably him; he's got size 10 feet!" she said, pointing at Cadogan.

"So what, loads of people have!" said Cadogan, wounded. "Sergeant Mendip does, Mr Belgeddes, even my mum. But I was the one who left the paint cans by the door, if I was going to rob the place, I would have moved them, wouldn't I?"

"It might be worth taking a look at their feet anyway, Sergeant," said Joe, who had been continuing the refurbishment in the background. "Presumably whoever walked through the paint in the boots and removed their shoes would have had to have left either in socks or barefoot, so there should be particles of paint..."

And then he stopped and thought.

"Actually Sergeant, no need. I know who stole the money and why."

Who does Joe Hollobone think committed the robbery?

Hint: One Set

11. Calling all Cars

Detective Inspector Radford was sometimes seen as a bit of an old-fashioned copper, which annoyed him as he'd only been on the force for about 15 years and he tried to embrace any and all modern developments, as long as they made his life easier. This included the existence of Constable Axton.

Therefore, when they began to bring in these new police 2-way radios Radford was very pleased, it was a great improvement on blowing a whistle or asking a constable to run to the station. Instantaneous communication! But it seemed to come with a near instantaneous problem.

It started at 8am in Guildford. The new radios received a call: 'Car Number 9 proceed immediately to number 3 Wodeland Avenue, a robbery is taking place!'

The policemen in Car 9 dutifully sped to the address and knocked frantically on the door, only managing to wake up a slumbering night watchman who informed them rather grumpily that there wasn't a robbery, and no-one had reported one.

It continued in the same vein: 'Car Number 16 to Guildford High Street, a lorry has crashed into the bank!' 'Car Number 10 to St John's Road, two individuals are involved in an assault on the street.'

Each time the policemen rushed to the scene and found there was no crime there at all. The calls kept coming, but now the policemen in the cars were torn. So far, they had all been false but what if one was real? Surely they had to keep investigating?

No-one knew who was sending the messages, especially as the system wasn't properly up and running yet. Was it a gang of crooks, using false reports to divert police from real ones, or maybe even report their own crimes knowing that the police would decline to investigate the boy who cried wolf?

"No-one recognizes the voice. No-one knows where it's coming from. But it's making us look like jackanapes," said Sergeant Longton. "Personally, I think the radio idea is a massive waste of time, but it's

Captain McDonald's pet project, he was very excited about the whole idea. He's in his office right now on some important business and I want to get this all squared away before he even knows it happened, or he'll be screaming in my earhole for days. What do you think, sir?"

"I'll have a look," said Radford. "Get me a car."

"It could be young people," said Constable Axton as he sat with DI Radford in Car 15.

"Amateur radio's the thing right now. My cousin Benjamin built his own, out of parts he ordered from a magazine..."

"The voice doesn't sound like kids," said Radford. "It's a man's voice, deep, maybe Scottish. Is there some kind of voice-changing microphone?"

Axton shook his head. "Could this be happening by accident? Like, it's a really bad poet who does...crime poems?"

Radford shook his head. "There's intent behind this. Let's go see Len Barstow."

Barstow was the local crime boss, the most approachable one, anyway, who maintained the front of being a respectable baker. As soon as they entered his bakery he broke into a big nasty grin.

"Hello hello hello! If it isn't the ghost chasers! Someone report this place is on fire, did they?"

Radford narrowed his

eyes. "Sounds to me like you know rather a lot about what's been happening today, Barstow."

Barstow opened an oven and began taking a loaf out. "You can't really miss it though, cars racing around, locals talking about how the peelers have gone mad."

"Do you have a radio, Mr Barstow?" asked Axton, trying to balance a currant bun on his index finger. "Or a Scottish accent?"

"Do I sound Scottish, young man?" said Barstow.

"Don't pretend you wouldn't benefit from us all running around like headless chickens," said Radford, annoyed at Barstow's flippancy.

"I'm just a simple baker," said Barstow. "But if I was involved in illicit activities, like you're implying that I am, having coppers zooming around, getting annoyed and worked up at having their time wasted would be a big problem because once you lot get a bee in your bonnet suddenly me and my lads are getting banged up on all sorts of false charges."

"You're the one making up crimes," said Radford, but he sounded less convinced. Barstow made a good point. One fake call would have provided cover for an actual crime, but this was just stirring up a hornet's nest. Maybe it was kids doing it.

Back in the car they heard another false message coming through, a supposed public nuisance at the park.

"Different crimes each time," said Axton thoughtfully.

"They really should have tested this system before they brought it online," said Radford, mulling whether to go to the park. Axton jumped up in his seat and banged his head on the car's roof.

"Ow! That's it sir. I know who's doing it!"

Mary hugged her back, but her mind had begun to turn things over.

"Celia, we need to think for a second. Are you certain it was your... fiddling with the car that caused the crash?"

Who does Constable Axton suspect of making the false radio calls?

Hint: Test

12. Strange Developments

One of Mary's friends, Thomas Hazelton, had recently taken up photography. He'd asked his friends to pose for portraits to use to drum up some business and Mary had obliged. She was so interested in the process that he'd allowed her to help him develop some of them in his dark room.

"Hang on a tic, that's a bit odd..." he said, looking at the negative. It was a picture he'd taken of her in the street on as she had looked happy and natural. But there was something happening in the window behind her that looked... worrying. He enlarged that part of the image and made a print.

"Does that look like... someone attacking someone with a knife?"

Mary peered at it. It was undeniable, there were some kind of shadowy figure, its blurred hands bringing a butcher's knife down on another shadow just visible, with a spray of what looked like blood erupting from the wound!

"Have we just accidentally witnessed a murder?" zsked Thomas.

"We had better find out," said Mary.

She thought it unlikely the police would act without more evidence. They returned to the street where the photo had been taken and worked out that the window had to be at the back of number 62, Leigham Court Road. At the moment the room seemed dark and unoccupied so they made their way to the entrance of the block.

It sat in an area that was somewhat run down but bustling with life, with a greengrocer, a butcher shop, and a haberdashery close by.

Thomas pushed the buzzer and after a delay the door opened a

crack; revealing two very large eyes in a pair of glasses with a large bushy moustache underneath.

"Can I help you?" Said a richly Irish accented voice, sounding friendly.

Thomas froze, unsure about how to say "we think someone was murdered in your house, possibly by you".

Mary stepped forward, "Hullo, we're here to see number 3?"

The man opened the door, looking confused. "I didn't know they were renting it. Mrs Hall didn't say anything about it."

"Oh, maybe we can talk to her and see if there's been a mistake?"

He seemed uncertain but let them enter the building. Inside it was very run down, with cracked walls and dusty corners.

"I'm Robert Murphy," the man said, rubbing marks off his apron. "I run the butcher's shop on the corner. It's small but we're expanding!"

"Do you often wear your apron at home?" Mary asked.

Murphy smiled. "I was just popping back to get my lunch. You're lucky I was here to answer the door, half the people in this building don't bother to answer it and the other half, like dear old Mrs Hall, aren't exactly what you might call speedy."

Looking at the layout of the building, Mary suspected the window they had seen was up on the third floor. Mrs Hall's apartment was on the second floor and Mr Murphy began knocking on it and shouting.

"MRS HALL? WERE YOU SEEING SOME TENANTS TODAY?"

"What's up there?" asked Mary. "We prefer higher floors."

The door to number 3 opened and a very grumpy looking old lady glared at them.

"What's this about tenants? I told that landlord I wasn't going anywhere! Is this your doing, Murphy? Bad enough you going up to number 4, carrying heavy things back and forth at all hours, dropping metal hooks in the stairwell."

"We said we wouldn't talk about that, Mrs Hall!" Murphy shouted.

Mary took advantage of the squabble that erupted between them to sneak up the stairs. There was only one apartment on the third floor, number 4, and its door lay tantalizingly open. She entered cautiously, finding it unlit, unfurnished, completely empty, and devoid of decoration, a shell. The heating was off, and it was freezing, which added to the haunting nature. No-one was inside, and when she found the room with the window, she had seen she found it even barer than the rest, with the floor stripped of any carpeting, with only bare dusty concrete. Despite the spartan appearance the place was evidently very clean, except for some rusty spots on the floor. Against her better judgement Mary touched one and then sniffed the dust, smelling the familiar coppery scent of... dried blood.

She was just noting that there were equally spaced holes in the ceiling when Thomas came into the room, followed shortly by a frowning Murphy.

"There you are darling!" said Thomas loudly, positioning himself in front of Mary.

"Oh yes, I was looking for the powder room," she said in a scatty voice.

"Well, it's not up here," said Murphy in a low voice that showed he didn't believe a word of it. He escorted them out, seeming more sad than angry, and then as they left the front door he leaned over to Mary and whispered.

"Please don't tell anyone what I did. They'll close the shop if they find out. I had to do it; I didn't have any choice."

And at that they left. Thomas' eyes looked as big as saucers.

"Well, I think our next port of call is the police station, see if anyone's gone missing locally." He said.

"No need," said Mary. "I know exactly what we saw."

What does Mary think happened in that room when the photo was taken?

Hint: Hooks

48

13. The Unbandaged Man

Joe Hollobone enjoyed doing repair work in museums as he had
a great interest in the minutiae of history, the tools and objects
people used in the past. He particularly enjoyed working at The Gregory
Huntmunson Museum in Arundel because the building itself was
almost an artefact, and he always tried to repair what was there while
preserving the original design and virtues of the charmingly small
museum, built in 1824 to house the collection of Gregory Huntmunson
himself. Its collection tended toward obscure Saxon artefacts and
occasional pieces from Asia. Hence the confusion when, as he was
getting ready to leave, an Egyptian sarcophagus arrived in a large crate!

Lois Nutt, the cleaning lady, gave Joe a confused look. He shrugged and
went to find the curator, Paul Keats, who he knew was working late.

"Oh yes, I was expecting this," he said. "We got a call from a Mr Omari
Mostafa! Apparently, his institute intends to gift this to our museum!
Flown by plane overnight. Very unorthodox, but who am I to complain?"

Keats eyed the sarcophagus, rubbing his hands together. Joe nodded
towards the crowbar in his toolbox.

"Want me to...?"

"Open it? This Mostafa chap said we have to wait for the presence
of a British Museum official before we can do that, said he'll be here
tomorrow morning. Such a shame..."

Joe shrugged and grabbed his tools, doffing his hat and leaving.

Therefore, he was surprised the next morning to find a police
car outside the museum. As he entered the building he saw the
sarcophagus, open and surrounded by police, and laid inside was not
an Egyptian mummy... but a dead man in modern clothing! He wore
a light shirt, partially unbuttoned, and linen trousers. His darkly
moustachioed face was fixed with an expression of terror.

"Ah, Joe," said Inspector Knatchbull, turning from the shocked looking
curator, Keats. "You were here last night when this arrived, correct?"

"He was!" Keats blurted out. "But he left before I...decided to open it."

"Shame, he could have been a witness," said Knatchbull. "We only have your word that when you opened it this man was inside."

"My word? But I... the body... Oh God!"

Keats covered his face and burst into tears.

"That reminds me, have we heard back from the museum?" Knatchbull asked a constable.

"Not yet sarge. Do you reckon this is the bloke they sent?" said the constable, peering at the corpse.

"We need to talk to this Mostafa. What's his number?" Knatchbull asked Keats. Keats seemed completely dazed.

"I... don't know... he never said. It was a very bad line, and he said there was a desert storm..."

Joe walked around the sarcophagus, taking a look at its construction. He was no Egyptologist, but it looked genuine to him. It did appear that someone had drilled a hole in the back, but it was gummed up with packing material from the crate. His shoes crunched on the ground, and he noted there was a thin layer of sand that had fallen from the coffin.

"Where's the mummy?" Joe asked.

Knatchbull shrugged. "No idea. All we know is the cleaning lady tells us she found Mr Keats here putting this body into the sarcophagus..."

"I wasn't putting it in!" Keats shouted. "It was already in there when I opened it this morning! I was just... looking for identification!"

"We checked, there isn't any," said Knatchbull to Joe conversationally. "No papers, no mummy, a strange situation."

Knatchbull had Keats taken back to his office to see if he could find

Mostafa's number and talked to Mrs Nutt, the cleaning lady again.

"I've always thought he was a wrong'un," she said, glaring at Keats' office. "Only got this job because he married the boss' daughter. Always talking to his bookie on the phone. Everyone thinks I'm deaf, but I hears it all. And he never had a cup of tea no matter how many times I offered!"

"There might be a reason for that, Lois," said Knatchbull sternly. "Remember what happened to your Eric?"

"That was natural causes, that was!" she said indignantly. "The coroner said so. What did this bloke die of anyway?"

"Suffocation and hypothermia, I should say," Joe remarked. "Bloodshot eyes and red patches on the face. But nothing around the neck, so not strangulation. And he's partially undressed himself, see the jacket on the floor of the coffin?"

Both Mrs Nutt and Sergeant Knatchbull raised their eyebrows at Joe's knowledge. He adjusted his glasses.

"Did you clean in here this morning, Mrs Nutt? The museum, I mean?" Joe asked.

"Not since I left last night. You think I'd leave sand on the floor?"

"I just noticed there's no bandages, or even bit of bandages. No drag marks either. And what do you make of these scratches?"

Joe pointed out a series of scratches on the inside of the sarcophagus.

"He was put in there alive, you think?" said Knatchbull, squinting. "Nasty way to go."

"I agree with almost everything you just said, Sergeant," said Joe. "And I know now who this man is and how he died."

What does Joe Hollobone think is the man's identity and cause of death?

Hint: Hypothermia

14. The Missing Claret Jug

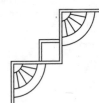

Radford gazed over the golf course in Jacob's Well, Surrey. He was partial to a game himself and some part of him was musing whether, if they wrapped this up quickly enough, he could get a quick 18 in before heading back to the station. He watched Constable Axton miming an invisible golf swing, somehow hitting himself in the face and falling over. No chance, he thought.

"Come on constable, Mr Leigh is waiting..." Radford shouted.

Fred Leigh was the president of Jacob's Well golf club. A prominent local businessman, he had used his connections to secure an exhibition of the Claret Jug, the famous trophy presented to the winner of The Open, as a way of increasing the prestige of his small club.

Normally on display at Royal and Ancient Golf Club of St Andrews, Leigh had arranged for the entire club to be renovated in anticipation of the Claret Jug's arrival. The clubhouse and golf course had been closed for two weeks while builders stripped out the entire contents and refurbished it. Radford could see from here that the entire building was covered in scaffolding, with only tarpaulins covering the windows.

"Unfortunately, the renovations are taking longer than planned because a couple of sandbags broke in there, so when the cup arrived yesterday, I couldn't display it," Leigh said, mopping his brow. "I put it in the safe in my office. Anyway, the builders have the day off today, but I went to check and found the safe open and the jug gone!"

"17,10,1860." Said Axton, who had somehow acquired a golf ball and was rubbing it against his ear.

Leigh went slightly pale. "How did you know the combination?"

"First date of the Open. When you said the safe was 'open' it occurred to me."

Leigh's lips moved without any words for a second. "I... didn't even think of that!"

"Also, you had it written behind the painting of Tandridge Priory," Axton continued.

"How did you..." said Leigh, stammering.

"Constable Axton looks behind every single painting he sees," said Radford wearily, remembering the recent art gallery burglary.

"I do! Also, there's a lot of sand in there, and I could see footprints just in front of the painting," Axton said, wandering off.

"Who is currently on the premises?" asked Radford.

"Well, the greenkeeper, Borodan Smith, he's mowing by the trees over there, then there's myself, and Frank Dittman." Leigh said, pointing to a similarly attired gentleman standing near one of the holes. Dittman gave them a short wave.

"And why are you here today, sir, considering the course is closed?" asked Radford.

"Dittman and I always play a game every March 26th, since I first beat him in 1923! It's a sort of unofficial tourney. I know the club's closed, but I couldn't not honour the date..."

"And you don't think anyone else could have gotten onto the premises?" asked Radford.

"No, we put in new fences, a new gate, everything was reinforced when we learned the jug was coming here. I hate to say it but... Our greenkeeper is in arrears on his rent. I should know, I played a round with his landlord last week! He's been bloody subordinate recently too, I asked him to go into the clubhouse to get some brandy and he just shook his head!"

Borodan Smith was a brooding, bulky man, breathing heavily he tended to the grass. He took big deep breaths between each statement, like he was holding something in.

"10 years I've worked here... Mr Leigh never complained before... I'd never steal from here..."

"But you've been having trouble paying your rent?" asked Radford.

"Put the rent up...not my fault...I work hard..."

Suddenly Smith had a coughing fit, sounding like he had trouble breathing. Radford moved to support him, but Smith held his hand up.

"I'm fine..." he spluttered, and strode off towards the woods, taking something out of his pocket that looked like a rubber bulb with something on the end and putting it up to his mouth with what looked like relief. Before Radford could do anything he suddenly noticed Axton was having a

mild altercation with Frank Dittman, Leigh's golfing partner.

"This... constable damaged my sand wedge!" said Dittman, pointing at Axton, who was holding his hands up in an attempt to mollify Dittman. "I'm glad I only brought half my clubs now, if this maniac is going to wreck them."

"Sorry sir, I was just seeing if sand stays on the end of it when you hit it against various objects." Said Axton.

"Why did you..." started Radford, and then just shook his head. "I'm terribly sorry sir, you'll be compensated."

"I should jolly well think so," said Dittman, hefting his heavy looking golf bag. "I have a meeting at 1 and I don't have time to dally around here forever."

"Mr Leigh said you play on this date every year?"

"Oh yes, Frank and I have been friends for a long time!" Said Dittman with a big smile that never reached his eyes.

"And you never went in the clubhouse today?"

"Why would it, bally thing's closed isn't it? Bit of a pain, normally we'll have a tipple between holes. Had to resort to the old pocket flask." Dittman said, waggling it in front of the detectives.

"There's sand on your shoes though," said Axton.

"That's from the bunker, constable, as I said!" said Dittman. "I accidentally teed off into there from the 5th hole. Leigh will tell you that. I hardly need to steal anything, Sergeant."

Leigh confirmed that Dittman had accidentally hit a ball towards the sand pit but hadn't personally seen him use the sand wedge to get it out, as he had felt a little queasy from the brandy they had been drinking and had had to sit down for a moment. "Dittman wouldn't steal the jug though, he has more money than I do! He's a shocking golfer, but a financial whiz."

Radford wandered over to the bunker and peered in. Axton followed him and Radford told him everything he'd found out.

"I don't think there's any chance of getting to play this course today, this is a tricky one," said Radford.

"Really? I'm pretty sure I know exactly who did it, sir," said Axton.

Who does Detective Constable Axton suspect of stealing the Claret Jug?

Hint: Wedge

55

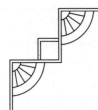

15. Who framed Bodger Mabbut?

66 Inspector Butler's here," said Ronson to Cynthia Croom.

"Is that how you're announcing yourself now, Ronson?" Croom asked him. "Most odd."

"No, not me madam, Inspector Butler from the police."

"Very well, show him in, perhaps he'll be a better butler than you."

Inspector Butler was a short, skinny man with moist cow-like eyes, entering Cynthia Croom's study with a look of awe.

"Croom Manor, my word! I never thought I'd get to see inside." Butler said, peering around the room.

"Are you a policeman or a tourist? What are you going to do about my painting?"

The police had received a call from Mrs Croom to say that her cornfield was missing. After some confusion it became apparent that she owned *The Cornfield*, a famous painting by Constable, and it had been stolen from her study.

"I kept it here, just above my desk," she said, indicating a space on the wall. Her study had a distinctive fleur-de-lis wallpaper and the painting had evidently been there so long that a medium-sized rectangular shape of a landscape painting was visible where the wall-paper, hidden from sunlight, had remained unfaded. There was no evidence of any break-in, so Butler suspected some kind of inside job.

"Do you distrust any of your staff, ma'am?" Butler asked.

"I distrust all of them!" Croom said thunderously. "Those lazy servants, that surly gardener, that insipid new girl the agency sent to help manage the estate! None of them were permitted to go into my study."

Butler immediately ordered his constables to find the Constable, which again caused some confusion, and they began with a search of the entire Croom estate. Butler himself decided to question the suspicious new girl.

"Now then Miss... Parnacki, has anyone approached you asking you to help steal a painting? Perhaps he promised you some jewels?" Butler said slowly.

"No, Inspector, I promise you I've heard no such thing. But I did notice…"

"Is this it sir?" said a policeman, showing Butler a medium sized painting of a Dutch village. "Found it propped up in the pantry."

"No, it's a cornfield, Johnson, put that back where you found it!"

Suddenly another constable ran into the room. They'd found the painting in the gardener's house!

"Bodger" Mabbut had a small cottage in the corner of the estate's famous Spanish Gardens, which he had carefully tended and maintained for almost 30 years. The constables had found the painting on display in his small living room and Mabbut had seemed surprised they were looking for it and even more surprised when they arrested him.

"The painting's mine!" he said to Butler when they brought him to the main house. "Mr Croom leave it me in his will!"

"Nonsense," said Cynthia Croom. "Oscar was cordial to you, certainly, he allowed for you to remain in the garden house even though you are now patently worthless for the job! But the idea that he'd give you a Constable!"

Mabbut opened his mouth to object, then closed it quickly. Butler narrowed his eyes, then nodded at the constable holding the painting in its ornate portrait-style frame…

"Constable, give the Constable to the butler. The Constable painting. And their butler, not me."

"…Sir? Isn't this evidence?" said the constable, struggling to hold the large painting.

"We don't need it; we already have the criminal! Take him to the station."

Miss Parnacki handed Inspector Butler a piece of paper.

"What's this?" he said.

"It's the number of the Croom family lawyer sir," she whispered. "I assumed you would want to contact him to check the details…"

"Check the details? Whatever for?" Butler said loudly. Miss Parnacki's eyes darted to look at Cynthia Croom, but she was too busy berating her butler Ronson (for not cleaning the muddy footprints the police were leaving everywhere) to hear them.

"I just thought that if for some strange reason Mrs Croom is wrong and Mabbut was bequeathed the painting it might be against the law to take it from him? I'm no expert of course…"

Butler opened his mouth to dismiss this foolishness but paused, then handed the number to a nearby constable.

"Check this out please Johnson," he muttered.

"I don't suppose there's any other tips you could give me about police work, Miss Parnacki." Butler said sarcastically.

"Oh, well, I assume you have interviewed Ronson, seeing as he used to be a burglar..." she said, apparently missing his tone.

"He what? I mean, obviously we're just about to speak to him."

Ronson was unapologetic. "I do indeed have a few misdemeanours in my past, sir, but I left them all behind me when I entered service and Mr and Mrs Croom have always known about it. In fact, Mrs Croom has been known to mention it in order to...keep me in line. I'm leaving here next week so I don't mind saying that."

Butler wasn't satisfied. "So, what was the idea, pinch the painting, stash it with your accomplice, let him take the fall if the scheme got rumbled?"

Ronson shook his head steadily. "I never go into Mrs Croom's study. For a butler to have such a blind spot about the house he runs has always been difficult for me, but I endured it. Therefore, I did not even know the painting existed."

Butler endured another conversation with Mrs Croom to find that she agreed that Ronson was unaware of the painting, and she knew he'd been a burglar, but she was convinced that it had been the gardener, even though she didn't trust the butler "a single jot!".

Butler went to sit down for a few minutes and gather his thoughts but before he could Constable Johnson returned to tell him that he'd been in touch with the family lawyer, a Mr Hector Judd, and he had nervously confirmed that the Constable painting had not been bequeathed to Mabbut.

"Well, that settles it," said Butler.

"It certainly does," said Miss Parnacki, loudly, from the doorway.

Who does Helen Parnacki suspect of stealing the painting?

Hint: *Size*

16. Pack of Thieves

This wasn't the most embarrassing evening Mary Fitzgerald had ever had but it was certainly in the running. When Sir James Mountstevens had asked her to perform at his venue, she had expected a ballroom full of people, not this dimly lit gambling club. She could kick herself for not recognizing the name of Crockford's. Hearsay had it Sir James was struggling financially so perhaps he thought some entertainment would liven up the venue?

Furthermore, Sir James seemed to have misunderstood the nature of her performances and so when she turned up ready to sing, he had hastily propped a microphone in the corner of one of the blackjack rooms, and she was dreading having to step over to it and begin warbling at all the people just trying to play cards. Wouldn't a singer be very distracting?

She was occupying her time staring at the players when suddenly one of them, a cadaverously thin older man, suddenly shot up in his chair.

"There is a criminal at this table!" he declared in a low, judgemental tone. "I should know, I am a high court judge." Which explained the tone at least.

"You, young lady, come here," he said, beckoning Mary with a skeletal finger. The other players at the table were simply glaring at him. "Can you write? I need someone to mark down my observations."

Mary had no interest in being this man's stenographer, but she was intrigued by his accusations. The table's dealer, a sharply dressed young woman named Alice, moved forward carefully.

"Please, perhaps we can discuss this in the office?"

But the judge, evidently named Reginald Bamstaff, ignored her entreaty and outlined his "case". He couldn't point to any particular player at the table as clearly winning more than they should, but the way that the cards were landing and the nature of people's hands and their frequency of going bust indicated to him that there was a card shark at the table.

"Card sharp, isn't it, not shark?" said Sophie DeLange, a society girl seated left of the judge. "Why would sharks play cards?"

"So, what is a sharp, then?" asked Meraldo Galfistoni, a recent immigrant to London who had been admitted to the club despite his scruffy yet surprisingly clean clothes.

Neither of them seemed particularly upset at being accused of cheating.

"I know you don't take me seriously; you think I'm just some sour old duffer," Bamstaff said, grimacing. "But I come here to enjoy the thrill of a game of chance, not to be led around like a pack horse."

"Well, no offence your worship, but seeing as

you're down about 20 pounds, a less charitable reading of this situation might be that you're flipping over the board when your king is in check, if you understand my analogy," said DeLange.

"Or perhaps it is he who sharpens the cards, and is looking to create an exit for himself," said Galfistoni.

"There are many ways one can cheat at Vingt-et-Un..." the judge continued, as if giving a ruling. "Marking the cards, interfering with the deck, and of course, should a dealer be slow or sloppy when they are checking their hole card, a confederate of the player can signal them with a noise or gesture!"

At this Bamstaff swung round on the spot to glare directly at a man standing by the door who was currently scratching his nose. He looked alarmed and held the finger away from him like it was a weapon.

"I, I..."

"Nigel works for me," said a plummy voice, and Sir James Mountstevens himself strode into the room. "I have in fact employed him to watch for possible cheats. I don't know why his nose is itchy."

He smiled apologetically at the assembled group, making his way round the room to ensure no-one was unhappy with the events, pausing to let Alice Capewell wipe a smudge of dust from his cravat and then approaching the judge carefully.

"Your worship, I'm satisfied there is no cheating going on here, if you have any other information, I would be glad to hear it..."

"Well, for example, Miss DeLange keeps reapplying her lipstick," The judge suggested.

"It keeps rubbing off on the cocktail glass," she said, "And it would make a

poor tool to mark the cards if that's your suggestion. I think your long fingernail would do a better job!"

She pointed at the extended, slightly curled nail on the judge's little finger.

"Ah yes, I am in fact an enthusiastic amateur lutenist. That is, I play the lute."

He mimed playing the lute. Mary reflected that she would rather have said she was a card cheat than admit that. She suddenly remembered that she had overheard two of the employees here complaining that cards had gone missing. But that was packs of cards, not individual cards, and therefore unlikely to have been stolen by customers. She decided not to mention it.

"I further suspect..." said the judge, his hands clutching his waistcoat, "That Signor Galfistoni here is not in fact a man of limited means but is in fact Count Geraldo Malfistoni, a young man of considerable breeding and means."

No-one seemed surprised at this except for Malfistoni who seemed very shocked at being revealed.

"It is true!" he gasped. "I have come here in disguise in order to find a woman who will love me for my heart, not for my lire."

And he gave Mary a big wink that made Sophie DeLange grimace.

Sir James came round the table between the judge and Miss Capewell. "I'm sorry sir, but nothing you have said has convinced me that anything untoward is happening here."

"Well, it has convinced me," thought Mary.

Who does Mary Fitzgerald think has been cheating at cards?

Hint: Cravat

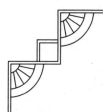

17. Shattered Faith

Joe Hollobone made it a principle not to involve himself in anything unless specifically asked. So, as he fixed the pulpit of St Alfeges Church in Greenwich, he was carefully ignoring Reverend Bosanquet's pacing and hand-wringing, which probably had something to do with the testy phone call he had had 10 minutes earlier.

"Do you... would you mind patching up the holes in our windows? Temporarily I mean. The man we usually use seems to be on holiday!"

Joe had noticed when he had entered that morning that parts of the church's stained-glass windows were broken. St George's dragon and the cross in the English flag, the blood in the grail, all the roses, completely smashed.

"The lord forgives all, Joe, but the wickedness of smashing our beautiful windows, it's inhuman. We are already short of money in the fund. And no-one has come forward to confess."

"I saw a few local kids hanging round the back," said Joe.

"Yes," said the reverend grimly. "That would be Charlie Partridge and his band of ne'er do wells. Notorious for causing mischief all around Greenwich, and now they've taken to hanging around the church. But I cannot immediately accuse them of smashing the windows, their parents would be outraged!"

"Who else?"

"Well, a sailor from one of the ships in the docks, some Greek fellow, he's been seen wandering about, looking for something supposedly. And then... well, I don't like to speak ill of my own flock, but Mrs Barchester took great umbrage at my sermon about purgatory and began berating me from the pews! She has an incredibly loud voice for an 83-year-old woman."

While the reverend hadn't directly asked him to look into the matter Joe had inferred it, so he headed out of the church and almost immediately bumped into a huge, weathered man with a wild beard and a worried expression. In his left hand he held a sack and under his right arm was tucked a piece of wood with what looked like a target with a red centre painted on it.

"Excuse me, sorry, have you seen... anything?" The man said in a thick Greek accent.

"You'll have to be more specific." Joe said.

"A little thing, maybe so big?" he said, holding his hands about a foot apart. "I don't want to say so much, I wasn't supposed to bring it and now it's gone."

Joe noticed he was holding a cloth sack and peered inside, wondering if it contained stones, but instead it had various pieces of bruised looking fruit. The sailor quickly closed the sack when he saw Joe peeking and, muttering, turned heel and headed towards the small park just behind the church.

Next Joe decided to pop in to see Mrs Barchester and after enquiring in the local greengrocer's found her home at the end of Burney Street. Her daughter invited him in and found her swathed in blankets in a tatty looking armchair, her eyes drilling into him as he explained he was collecting donations for a restoration fund for the windows.

"The nerve of that man!" seethed Mrs Barchester, knocking her cup of tea on the floor. "First he blasphemes on the pulpit and now he wants more money for his church!"

"What did he say?" asked Joe, squeezing tea out of his sleeve.

"He said hell and purgatory dwell below us! How dare he! Every good Christian knows hell and purgatory live right here among us, in the corners and cracks of this sinner's paradise!"

Joe saw Mrs Barchester's daughter roll her eyes in the doorway.

"And now you hate St Alfeges?" He asked.

"St Alfeges is gone, as far as I'm concerned, in its place only a den of iniquity! I've seen omens of its downfall too! I saw a tiny hairy-faced demon in the graveyard, a malevolent hobgoblin!"

"Charlie Partridge?" asked Joe. A ball of wool suddenly hit his foot and he realized that she had tried to throw her knitting in his face.

"GET OUT! BLASPHEMER! ICONOCLAST!" she yelled, and her daughter escorted him out.

"Charlie's her godson," the daughter said by way of apology, then slammed the door in his face.

Joe now returned to the church, and with the modicum of stealth that he still retained from his criminal days he managed to use the cemetery's many trees to sneak up behind the three small boys trying to hide in the graveyard. They jumped out of their skins and two of the boys gazed at him with looks of terror while the third slightly bigger boy squared up to him with a look of defiance, quickly hiding something behind his back.

"What do you want?" he said.

Joe wordlessly looked up at the broken stained-glass windows. Charlie looked at them too then back at Joe.

"Wasn't us," he said.

"We're just looking for the..." started a smaller boy, then he shut up with a yelp when Charlie gave him an elbow. As Charlie moved Joe could see what he was holding in his hands behind his back: a bag of peanuts still in their shells.

"Looking for the what?" he asked.

"Nothing, we haven't heard nothing," Charlie said, and at his urging the three boys ran out of the graveyard toward the park, peering up at the trees as they went.

Joe returned to the church and the fretting Reverend.

"I know who broke the windows," he told him. "Although you might not believe me!"

Who does Joe Hollobone suspect broke the stained-glass windows?

Hint: *Fruit and nuts*

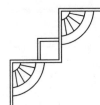

18. A Sign of Character

Sergeant Grimsdale shook his head as he looked at the hole in the fence. He'd warned the property owners that children were going to keep sneaking into the abandoned factory and messing around, hurting themselves and each other, but they clearly hadn't listened and now a young lad was lying unconscious in hospital with a goose egg on the back of his head and a wailing mother by the bedside.

The owners of the derelict building clearly had no respect for the seriousness of this situation because they had sent some clueless young woman, a Miss Parnacki, to talk to him. As he came through the gates, he saw her peering up at the old building, with its sign reading "H BERT CONFECTIONARIES". Sergeant Grimsdale had marched up to her and told her what was what.

"Now listen here young lady, I can tell you exactly what happened here. Three local lads have been coming here for some tomfoolery. Tom and Adam Coddle and Billy Bramhall, I know them well. There's a hole up by the canal where the factory overhangs it. Well, this morning the younger Coddle boy and Bramhall came into the station and told me that Tom had snuck in on his own and they had found him lying right in front of the entrance with a massive lump on his head."

Miss Parnacki covered her mouth in alarm. "Oh, my goodness! How was he hurt?"

"Well, here's the rum thing. When Adam Coddle was out of earshot, little Billy said that when they found Tom, he had looked at his brother, and said 'It was you!' just before he passed out!"

"Oh no! So he hit his brother?"

"Seems so, but don't think that gets your company out of trouble young lady! He could easily have bonked him on the head with a brick or a bit of wood from this building."

He surveyed the old factory. Twenty years ago, Hubert's Confectionaries had been the heart of the community, employing a lot of local people, but the decline in the popularity of its products meant it had shut down about 2 years ago, and the building had already been shoddily maintained by then. Now it was a death trap and people were constantly complaining about finding bits of it in the canal, one fisherman claiming he'd almost been brained by a dislodged brick.

"So you can tell your bosses from me that…"

"Oh, um, I'm sorry Sergeant but they don't actually know I'm here! I was told to call you on the phone and tell you they would look into it, but I thought, um, it would be better if someone came and had a look."

Grimsdale frowned. He couldn't quite get the measure of this girl. She knelt down on the tiled path that led to the entrance, touching a spider-web like crack on one of the tiles.

"When might it have happened, do you think?" she asked him without looking up.

"Well, their mother said the boys had their supper last night and went to bed at the usual time. She swears they couldn't have snuck out and I have no reason to doubt her. The boys might be a bit wild but Mary Coddle is a reliable woman. Anyway, she sent Tom, the injured boy, off with a note for the butcher's at 8:15am, and then Billy Bramhall calls for Adam and the two of them go off."

"And then Adam left Billy, met his brother in the factory and hit him?"

"That's what I reckoned, but Billy claims he was with Adam the whole time! He might be covering for him, but then why did he dob him in when he got the chance!"

"Maybe he changed his mind?" she said. "Or he was afraid of Adam?"

"No... Adam Coddle's a bit of a rascal but he's not a bad boy as such. None of them are."

"Did the doctors say anything about Tom's injury?"

"Nothing too serious but he'll be in there a week or two they reckon. A hard knock, right from above. I suppose when the boy wakes up, we'll have the truth of it. All else he's said is something about getting a letter, but his mum said they haven't had any post recently. It had to have been his brother."

"It couldn't have been...," said a tentative little voice. Sergeant Grimsdale and Miss Parnacki wheeled round to see a grubby little boy standing nervously nearby with his hands behind his back. "I was watching them the whole time they was playing before they found Tom. Billy never left Adam at no time."

"Norman Pitkin!" the sergeant exclaimed, crossing his arms. "What were you doing spying on those boys?"

"Nothing bad I swear! I was playing science, I got this magnet out of the canal and I wanted to see if I could magnetism a coin out of Billy's pocket, I know his mum gave him it for the greengrocer! I was going to give it back after but the magnet don't work anyway."

Miss Parnacki knelt down next to him.

"Can I see the magnet?"

He brought it out from behind his back and showed her. She nodded and then showed it to Sergeant Grimsdale.

"Well, there we go. It's obvious who is responsible for Tom Coddle getting knocked on the head."

Who does Helen Parnacki suspect of being responsible for Tom Coddle's injury?

Hint: Letter

The two young men surveyed the richly appointed dining room. Lord Granston Rustin had told Fred Digby they should solve the theft without the involvement of the police.

"We don't need their clomping boots messing up the dining room," he sneered.

"Shouldn't our first suspect be, um, you know?" said Digby, pointing at the cleaning lady working in the corner.

"The staff are carefully vetted. And well paid, probably better than they should be! Anyway, that is Helen Parnacki. Rogerson and Harris saw her cleaning the chapel at 6:30 so she couldn't have done it."

Rustin beckoned her over.

"I heard somewhere you know shorthand, is that right?"

"Um, yes sir, from my previous employment."

"I was just thinking we needed someone to take some notes. Did you hear about the missing tin of pâté?"

Miss Parnacki's eyes went wide, and she leaned forward. "Is it true that it was... dodo pâté?"

Digby and Rustin nodded. They were members of St Maximus' famous "Trencherman's Supper Club", a group that met bi-annually to eat "rare and exotic dishes and animals". Founded in 1847, Rustin was its current chairman, partly because he was a well-regarded chap, but mainly because he was the great grandson of the club's founder.

The club wasn't as prosperous as it once had been. Decades ago, there'd been memorably bizarre feasts of tiger pie and boiled elephant trunk but recently it had been "arctic" fox stew that turned out to be regular Reynard, and escalopes made from a penguin suspected to have been kidnapped from London zoo.

The supper club's feasts were usually spearheaded by Giuseppe Beretti, a chef who worked for a number of different supper clubs in Oxford, although he always claimed he preferred the Trencherman's club over them all. He proved it by bringing them something incredible:

He had purchased a tin containing the world's last known portion of dodo pate!

"It will make the perfect conversation piece!" he smiled.

"Conversation piece my foot!" said Rustin. "It shall be our main course. We have to taste dodo!" And the other assembled club members nodded enthusiastically.

But Beretti hadn't intended it to be opened and was extremely unhappy about the idea of serving anything from a tin, even if it was extremely rare and old.

"Why don't I just give you all... baked beans from the 16th century!"

He had shouted at the group, and when swotty Jenkins pointed out the canned food process wasn't invented until the early 19th century he stormed out in a huff.

But he changed his mind, and when Beretti arrived at the kitchen at 6:30 (before any of his other staff) to begin preparing the meal he found the can missing.

"Who else had been present in the building?" asked Miss Parnacki, scribbling frantically.

"Oh well, Digby and I, actually. Beretti invited us to come early so that we could have the first taste of dodo before all the other chaps stuck their snouts in the trough."

Digby was a new addition to the club, no pedigree at all but his father owned a brace of factories in the North and had decided to buy his family some class with an Oxford education. Rustin liked Digby's charming naivety and bulging wallet, so he was currently his best chum.

"Was anyone else here?" Miss Parnacki asked. The young men both shook their heads. "Do you think someone could have broken in?" she asked further.

"Not likely, all the locks here have been reinforced since the incident when Brasenose snuck in to steal the college cups," Rustin said. Inter-college rivalry was at a fever pitch this year. There had even been a few nasty rumours amongst the club about Digby being an infiltrator from another college, but Rustin had instructed the group to pay them no mind.

"Well then sirs, I don't mean to be rude, but, um..." Miss Parnacki paused. "It seems that only you two and Signor Beretti had the opportunity to take the tin."

Rustin paused, his mouth open.

"By Jove she's right!" Digby exclaimed. "We're the only suspects!"

"Well then it must have been Beretti," Rustin said quickly. "He

didn't want to serve from a tin, so he just tipped it in the trash and pretended there'd been a thief."

All three of them rushed to the kitchen and perused the rubbish bin. Nothing but potato skins and some very rancid smelling sardines. Beretti was actually standing there with his arms crossed, looking annoyed. Rustin and Digby rounded on him.

"Listen Beretti, where did you put the tin?" said Rustin. "I know you think you're a cordon bleu chef but if we don't eat the pate then it's this club that'll go the same way the dodo did in 1861!"

"1681," muttered Digby, and then Rustin suddenly turned to glare at him.

Now Rustin turned to look at Digby. "You're suddenly very knowledgeable about these things! Why are you such a Dodo expert? Maybe you were sent to steal it by Brasenose!"

"That's not very fair, Rusty!" Digby said.

"That's Lord Rustin to you." he said, puffing up his chest. "I'm just saying that I'm the only person here who had no motive to filch the tin."

"Is that so?" said Digby, suddenly seeming a little more sly. "I heard that you owe 50 pounds to Kendall Minor after a shockingly bad game of Backgammon."

"Surely neither of you could have stolen it if you were together," said Miss Parnacki, looking confused.

"Actually, I went off to get some Chateau Petrus from the cellar, Beretti said it'd be just the ticket to go with the pate," said Rustin. "So Digby was unattended!"

"So were you," Digby said. "I went to get the glasses."

Miss Parnacki suddenly closed her notebook and clapped her hands. "OK boys," she said to the three assembled young men. "I know who took the pate."

Who does Helen Parnacki suspect of stealing the tin of dodo pate?

Hint: Centuries

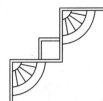

20. Garden of Horrors

Joe Hollobone was happily working at the Royal Botanic Gardens in Kew, restoring the Palm House. It was very humid inside the Palm House (due to the many tropical species of plant), but it was also beautiful and peaceful.

He hadn't told his employers that his Palm House expertise came from the time he had planned to steal seven rare orchids from the building.

Suddenly he heard a volley of cries and protests in the distance. He left the House and headed towards the commotion.

It was coming from the Jodrell Laboratory, a small facility where research was conducted, and the more unusual new plant arrivals were inspected before being transferred to the main Gardens.

He entered the central room to find scientists and other personnel gathered round a very strange looking plant. It seemed like a cross between a Venus flytrap and an avocado, bigger than a man, bulbous and vibrant green, with a mass of darker green leaves beneath it and visible white roots within a big trough of soil.

The people seemed undecided between attacking or protecting the plant. As Joe entered a man that he recognized as Thomas Netherton, one of the chief botanists there, turned to him and spoke.

"The Dionaea Corpusla has eaten Felicity Barbas!"

Apparently last night the botanists at Kew had received an unexpected arrival: The biggest carnivorous plant ever recorded! It arrived at the gates without any advance warning from the tropical jungle of Nicaragua. No-one had even phoned ahead. Felicity Barbas, a low level member of the botany team, had signed for the delivery and then immediately phoned Dr Netherton to come and inspect the specimen, but Netherton had insisted that it could wait and asked her to simply remain there and ensure it was kept healthy and... fed. Imagine their surprise when upon arrival this morning staff had told Netherton that Barbas disappeared, and then when he had cautiously examined the plant he could see inside... a large human shape.

Netherton held a lantern behind the huge central pod, and everyone assembled could clearly see a man (or woman!) sized shadow in the plant.

"Cut it open then," Joe said flatly.

The assembled group pulled a variety of sour faces.

"That's the thing..." Netherton said. "...there has never been a find like this in the history of botany! Damaging this incredible plant in any way would be a terrible crime!"

"But if she's inside..." said one of his colleagues.

"Oh yes, of course, human life takes priority. I just think we have to, ahem, be 100% sure she is in there!"

"You're just chasing headlines again," muttered a short bespectacled botanist. "You're probably thrilled it ate her; this will be on all the front pages by this afternoon."

"Have you touched the plant?" Joe asked, moving toward it. "Felt the weight without damaging it?"

Netherton stepped in front of him. "That's impossible I'm afraid. The paperwork explains that the central lobes, the uh, 'mouth', are covered in tiny sticky hairs that cause extreme irritation and soreness to the human body. No doubt a mechanism to prevent exactly the kind of rescue that we are contemplating."

"So who saw her last?" Joe asked, peering as close as he could. The plant's surface did indeed seem to have some kind of irregular black filaments on it.

"That would be me as well." Netherton continued. "I was giving her some supportive guidance..."

"Balderdash!" said an older botanist with a walrus moustache. "You've been bullying the poor gel for weeks. Disputing her observations, questioning her integrity. You've applied to the board to have her dismissed. All just because she disputed your assessment!" The other botanists mostly nodded.

Netherton bristled at this. "Science thrives on rigorous scrutiny, and I apply that equally to all of you. It's not my fault her work is shoddy. And she has allowed that journalist beau of hers into the facility several times without authorisation, let's not forget that!"

He suddenly thought of something and turned to Joe. "In fact, how do we know that this fellow wasn't here last night? I know he's been frustrated that his paper is doing badly. I visited his house to warn him off coming here and he had stacks of old newspapers inside! Perhaps he got into a fury and tipped her into the plant himself? You should look into his background."

"Why would I do that?" asked Joe. "I'm just a repairman."

Netherton looked baffled. "You're not a police detective? I just assumed... Then why the blazes am I talking to you?"

A few of the other botanists left the room saying it was too stifling, even though the room itself was colder than other rooms in the facility.

"You can leave sir, I'm sure, but I feel one of your colleagues might take a machete to the plant in your absence," said Joe, and Netherton begrudgingly accepted the point. "Do you have an alibi for last night?"

"I was at home with my wife."

"How do we know you haven't just bumped her off the old-fashioned way and are just pretending she's in there?" said walrus-moustache, pointing accusingly.

Dr Netherton sighed. "If I had come here, Harold would have seen me," he said, nodding to the nearby nightwatchman. "Did you see me last night, Harold? Or this journalist chap, Philip Grey, I think he's called?"

"Neither." Harold mumbled. "All I know is at 11:40pm this truck pulls up, a bit small for a delivery truck, and then Miss Barbas comes with a scissor-lift trolley and puts the box on it from the back. I offer to help but she says it's very delicate, then she wheels it off to the lab and the truck drives off."

Joe considered this, and then carefully took a craft knife from his tool kit.

"I understand now," he said and plunged it towards the plant pod very casually.

What does Joe Hollobone suspect has happened to Felicity Barbas?

Hint: Papers

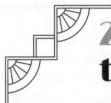

21. Hard to Convey

"It's a real tragedy," said John Downing, looking at the mangled wheels and torn rubber of the broken conveyor belt.

"Oh, don't worry," said Miss Parnacki, who had been asked to be the factory's unofficial liaison with Downing. "There were only a few injuries, and they were not too serious."

"I mean the RXF-23B!" he said, pointing at the machine. "This was her first outing in a real factory, and someone's nobbled her!"

"You suspect sabotage?"

Downing nodded fiercely. "The RXF-23B wouldn't break this badly unless someone messed with it."

The new conveyor belt had been gifted to the Almond's Cherry Pies factory by Wright & Downing in a mutually beneficial publicity move, allowing the factory to boast about its new technology, and W&D to promote their new products.

However, shortly after the belt was installed W&D and Gregory McNamara (the factory's new owner) had fallen out when the manufacturers claimed he owed them money for the device when he thought it was completely gratis.

The conveyor belt's design allowed workers to each man a station for their particular role in the pies' construction, from producing the filling, to making the crusts, and putting them in the tins for cooking.

Two hours ago, it had suddenly stopped, and then collapsed, its rubber belt snapping and the mechanical workings bursting out in all directions.

No-one present said that they had seen anything unusual happening before the conveyor broke.

Mr Downing quickly located the source of the problem: A mangled up pie-tin jammed in the works. "Unbelievable! Who was working on it when it broke? This was a criminal act!"

Miss Parnacki peered at the rota. "Um, William Kenneths, he's the foreman, then Sally Green, Marjory Cook, and up at the end Agnes Sudwell, and, oh... Mr McNamara."

Downing looked incredulous. "McNamara working on the factory floor?"

"He said he wants to muck in with the workers. if I'm honest, I think he just likes conveyor belts…"

"Or he just sabotaged so he could claim it was defective. Or got one of the others to do it."

"Well, it wasn't Archie Green or Kate Cook, several other workers were near them at the time it broke, and they said they didn't see anything." Miss Parnacki said, suddenly leaning down. She picked up a pair of scissors, and what looked like a pentagonal piece of striped silk amongst the gears.

"Look at these," she said, but Downing was uninterested.

"Arts and crafts. Do you have any more insights?"

"Well, the foreman, Mr Kenneths, he might lose his job soon, as they're looking to reduce the number of workers here now that they have…had…the conveyor belt. And Agnes Sudwell has…well there are a lot of stories from workers here about her behaving strangely. Talking to herself, carrying around sharp objects for no reason."

"Well, that's concerning, but I want to talk to Mr McNamara." Downing said, marching up to the main office.

Inside the office, McNamara looked unhappily at the spanner, rubbing his neck. Miss Parnacki noticed he wasn't wearing a tie, very unusual for him.

"Maybe it was an accident?" said McNamara eventually.

"Do your workers often wave spanners around while making pies??" Downing shouted.

"I don't appreciate your tone, Mr Downing. That conveyor belt was defective! And you fit it too low, people had to bend over to use it…"

"But the spanner, sir," said Miss Parnacki. "Do you think it might have been Mr. Kenneths? Or Mrs Sudwell?"

"Not Mrs Sudwell," said McNamara suddenly. "Please don't go around accusing our staff of sabotage, young lady."

Downing then decided to talk to William Kenneths, who was currently nursing a bandaged finger while sipping tea, a couple of visible spots of blood on the overalls that he (and all factory workers) wore.

"That...thing was a menace even before it broke," he said sorely, glaring at Downing. "I couldn't have chucked a spanner in there though, I was standing back and supervising, nowhere near the gears. I heard a sudden strangled cry of pain, then the whole thing seized up and collapsed and a spring sliced my finger open." He held up his hand to demonstrate.

"A cry before it broke?" asked Miss Parnacki. Who was it?"

"I don't know, sounded like a man."

"Where's this Agnes Sudwell?" asked Downing tetchily.

"Mr McNamara sent her home, gave her the day off. I don't think she was even injured!"

Downing insisted on being taken to see her and luckily her house was very close. She answered the door still in her overalls, looking at them with surprise and suspicion, especially when Downing asked about her strange conduct.

"The doctors have a fancy name for it, but I've just called it my brain fog," she said. "My instincts are still sharp when they need to be."

"Why did Mr McNamara send you home?" Miss Parnacki asked.

"...Gratitude," said Mrs Sudwell and wouldn't be drawn further.

As they left the house Downing loosened his tie with frustration. "Brain fog? Well, I haven't the foggiest what actually happened!"

"I do," said Miss Parnacki. "I know exactly who did it, and why."

Who does Helen Parnacki suspect of throwing the pie-tin into the machinery, and why?

Hint: Papers

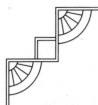

22. The Great Train Robbery

"The Flying Scotsman has been stolen!" Radford declared as he and Axton raced to Guildford Train Station.

"But it's a London to Edinburgh train, sir, what was it doing in Guildford?" Axton asked, driving even more recklessly than usual.

"Everyone knows the usual route, Constable. Apparently, they're making a sequel to that Flying Scotsman film there."

They arrived at the station and headed for the film's set, which was being built at a disused branch-line.

"Who's in charge here?" Shouted Radford.

A stout man in a crisp looking suit stepped forward. He looked extremely tired.

"I'm Robert Stephenson," he said.

"Like the inventor of the Rocket?" interrupted Constable Axton.

Stephenson rolled his eyes. "A distant relative. Please be discreet, Inspector. If the press gets hold of this it'd be very difficult for both us and London & North Eastern."

The Flying Scotsman was the flagship locomotive for the LNER line and had been lent to the production company on the understanding that the twin scrutiny of both the company's crew and the management at Southern Railways (who operated the trains on this line) would ensure its safety. There was also the train's actual crew, and several people from LNER's publicity department.

"All these people and somehow the train vanished?" Radford asked, watching Axton wander off towards the broken-down locomotives that were being stored in the sidings.

An energetic, thin fellow put his hand up.

"I'm Tolliver Pink, the director! A film set is a bustling whirl of activity, Inspector, so combined with the operations of this station, everyone thought someone else was watching her and then this tragedy occurred."

"But the film is about the train, right?" Radford said with incredulity.

"Actually, the studio's new American owners heard the words 'Flying Scotsman' and thought it was about planes! Philistines," said Pink sourly.

"The 4472 is a beautiful miracle of engineering! I thought I'd be riding it around for weeks! But we're just doing a few scenes with her here and then we're off to shoot for a month on something called a 'De Havilland Flamingo'."

"Not if you don't locate that ridiculous train!" said Stevenson to Pink, prodding him with a scrubbed red forefinger, before suddenly backing off and thrusting his hands in his pockets.

The Scotsman had arrived at 6:15pm the previous day and been put in the sidings ready for filming the next day. Everyone was staying in the nearby Railway Arms and Stephenson had treated them to a slap-up dinner, so the station had been locked up just after the last train came through at 10.59pm by the Stationmaster, Ronald Dankworth.

"Dankworth? As in Donnie Dankworth?" said Radford.

Donnie Dankworth ran half the criminal outfits in Surrey and was in the middle of taking over the other half when he was thrown into Pentonville Prison for tax evasion.

"I was his brother," said a surprisingly small bespectacled man in a station master's cap. "But not anymore, as far as my family are concerned. If you think I stole the locomotive for my brother you're on the wrong track."

Dankworth had discovered the Scotsman was missing the next morning, along with the assistant stationmaster and several porters.

"All the other engines that were supposed to be in the sidings were present, according to the manifest," Dankworth said. "I'm very good with numbers. But I could immediately tell the Scotsman had gone, that Darlington Green livery really made it stand out against the standard black of our normal engines. That's when we discovered the hole in the fence!"

He pointed at the hole in question, over by the stored engines.

"No doubt some thugs broke in and made off with it," Dankworth said.

"You can't just 'make off' with a steam locomotive!" Radford said. "You have to be able to operate it!"

This was clearly a professional theft, thought Radford, which also explained why no-one had witnessed the Scotsman leaving the

station. He had hoped that some member of the public might have seen it running along the line last night or this morning, but they had received no reports.

"The hole was cut from the inside," Axton said casually.

"What?" said Stephenson wearily. "How can you tell?"

Axton went to talk but Radford held his hand up. "He can tell," he said. "Who else had the keys to the station?"

"Because of the Scotsman we confiscated all other keys except for mine and Mr Stephenson's," Dankworth said. "Although Mr. Pink did insist on having some because he said the film set is technically property of the production company and he couldn't be denied access."

"Is that correct, Mr. Pink?" Stephenson said. "You could have hopped into the Scotsman and taken a chance to 'ride it around', as you said. Maybe you crashed it somewhere!"

"You'd like that, wouldn't you, Stephenson?" said Pink. "Then your rival's number one train would be out of commission? Anyway, I don't have time to take joy rides, I'm dealing with multiple production issues. You can see that the set is barely finished!" Pink indicated a small shack that was clearly made of plywood, where a young man was applying black paint. He looked annoyed.

"It's not my fault Mr Pink, we're missing many tins of paint." the boy said.

"First trains, now paint," muttered Stephenson. "It's not exactly the Bank of England here, is it Dankworth?"

"Oh, don't worry sir," said Axton. "I know exactly where the Flying Scotsman is."

Where does Constable Axton think the Flying Scotsman is, and who stole it?

Hint: Paint

23. Vicious Cycle

Mary loved Soho. While some could find it menacing or run down, she only saw the artists and musicians who wandered the streets and filled the cafes and pubs with laughter and passionate discussion.

She had managed to secure a nightly spot at a very small nightclub. One Friday she was leaving the club when she saw a cyclist riding at some speed brushing against a young man walking along the road. She noticed the bicycle more than the rider, a vivid blue–green colour, but once the cyclist had passed, the man suddenly cried out and clutched his legs. Mary ran over to see that his trousers now had slashes in them, with several deep cuts in his legs!

She walked him to the Middlesex hospital in Windmill Street where a friendly nurse greeted the sight of his wounds with "Not another one!"

Five other people had been brought in with leg lacerations. Mary concluded that the only thing all the victims had in common was they had been walking around Soho in the past couple of hours.

Mary would not tolerate this.

Leaving the hospital, she returned to the scene of the crime and secured the help of a friendly young bobby on the beat named Constable Rossini. He looked horrified when she described the crimes.

"You're in luck actually" He exclaimed. "I'm a bit of a connoisseur of bicycles. I'm always spotting interesting ones around this area. If I recall correctly there's only three people I can think of who have blue–green bicycles…"

The first was a local postman, Brian Roth. He was a bit notorious for having a little too much to drink and being a bit late with his deliveries.

"I know his bike by sight, he's fallen off it enough times! Actually, earlier Mrs Jones at the tobacconist wanted me to collar him for running his bike into the sign outside her shop this morning!"

When they knocked on his front door he was swaying slightly, and it took him a few seconds to realize Rossini was a policeman.

"Is this about the sign?" he said quickly.

"Possibly, sir," Rossini said in a very level voice. Do you own a green-blue bicycle?"

"Yes, have you found it?" Roth said, having trouble focusing. "I left it round the back, and it's gone."

"When did this supposed theft occur, sir?"

Roth shook his head as if to clear it. "I dunno, an hour ago?"

He brought them both round to show them the absence of bike, then staggered back inside, apparently passing out on his sofa 30 seconds later.

"I'm not sure I believe his story," Rossini said. "But he's not the slashing type. Now, our next contestant, however..."

Mickey "Knives" Niven was a local go-between for various gambling dens and other underworld figures. He'd never been caught doing anything illegal, but all the locals knew his frequent bike trips weren't between the pet shop and the church. They found him on the corner of Great Marlborough Street, leaning against his blue-green bike and giving Rossini a cynical sneer. Rossini peered round him to see if there were any blades on the wheels and Knives moved round to block his view.

"Don't reckon you're going to get one of these on a copper's salary, mate," he said. "I'll take you for a ride though, love."

"Someone's been slashing people's legs with a bicycle, Knives, and Constable Rossini is checking wheels," said Mary sharply. "Do you have something to hide?"

Knives looked a bit less smug and stepped to the side, revealing with a flourish that his wheels had no blades on them.

"There, happy? I ain't got time to go round cutting strangers. That's more like your lot. I've heard some terrible things..."

"Why do they call you Knives, then?" Rossini asked, unamused as he peered at the wheel.

Knives rolled his eyes. "It's my surname, Niven, isn't it? Sammy Hawkshaw started it as a joke. Ha bloody ha."

Rossini decided they should check out their third suspect before he arrested anyone. However, he thought it was unlikely that Philomena Winsop would be awake at this time of night, and he was reluctant to wake her up. Mary didn't necessarily blame him, even if he was supposed to be a brave policeman. She'd seen this woman wheeling her bicycle around Soho, handing people pamphlets about the dangers of jazz and the sinfulness of the blues from its basket. Her eyes blazed with righteousness.

"Maybe we can just check her bicycle without knocking on her door?" He said. Mary gave him a stern look and he shrugged and banged on the door sharply. Philomena Winsop answered surprisingly quickly, her face a mask of fury before she put her glasses on and saw that it was a policeman.

"Oh, an officer of the law! Well, it's not exactly a reasonable hour but virtue never sleeps! Have you come to join my crusade?"

"Not exactly. Can I see your bicycle?"

She looked confused, briefly offended, but then opened her door and wheeled it out to show him. There were crudely drawn pictures of the planet on the wheels, but no blades.

"You see, they represent the circle of life, the wheel of piety that has been broken by that monstrous music they call Jazz!" She hissed this last word, then suddenly peered at Mary.

"Do I know you?"

"No..." Mary said, although there was something about what she'd said that made her think.

"So you want to hurt people who like Jazz?" Rossini asked, carefully.

"No! I want to save them!" Winsop gushed. "Their souls are in torment; they must be freed!"

Rossini nodded towards Mary, then ushered her out of Philomena's hearing range.

"I think we know who the Soho Slasher is," he said.

"Yes, I think we do," Mary said, although she was fairly certain it wasn't for the reason Constable Rossini thought.

Who does Mary Fitzgerald suspect is the 'Soho Slasher', and why?

Hint: *Crash*

24. Quid's In

"Thieves," said Mr Twill,** his dry lips pursed characteristically. "It is our job to winkle them out. Some abhor the mugger, the street thug, the cut-purse, but in my estimation the basest wretch of all... is the embezzler!"

His staff all nodded. They had heard the speech before but knew not to interrupt their chief auditor.

"A mugger or hooligan might temporarily inconvenience a single citizen, but the embezzler steals the very life blood of industry. The embezzler is a vampire. And he will be brought into the light."

Helen Parnacki (junior auditing assistant third grade) thought it ironic that someone as pale and cadaverous as Mr Twill would call anyone else a vampire. But she did find this audit interesting.

The firm of Tompkins, Butterworth and Twill had been hired by the Dearmans & Son's shoe factory to comb their books for evidence of embezzlement.

The reason? Norman Phripps, the company's normally mild-mannered bookkeeper, had suddenly begun acting like a Hollywood movie star. He had bought an expensive new car. He wore a new wardrobe of fashionable clothes, initially stylish black suits before transitioning to more colourful ensembles. He was seen visiting nightclubs and concerts with Lilly Parsons, the secretary of the factory's owner, Sir Cedric Dearmans.

"If he is embezzling, is it not supremely stupid to be spending so ostentatiously?" asked Huggins, one of the other auditors.

"A fair point," Twill declared. "But he would not be the first embezzler to act like a foolish peacock."

"Or a peahen," said Miss Parnacki quietly. The other young auditors scoffed at this, but Mr Twill quieted them with a look.

"Miss Parnacki is quite correct," he said. "We must not let our affection for the more delicate sex blind us to the possibility that it is the secretary girl Miss Parsons who is stealing the company's funds!"

"But he's the one spending the money," said Tribble, a fastidious young auditor.

Twill made a dismissive noise. "The girl could simply have passed the money to him, knowing his weakness for expenditure would make him seem the guilty party if any investigation took place. And then of course, there is Owen Dearmans, Sir Cedric's son."

Owen had in the past been dissolute and a bit of a gambler, but he had returned from 3 years in the antipodes, working for a mineral excavation and extraction company in New South Wales with a self-declared determination to prove himself in the business as a shrewd investor. His father's trust wasn't so easy to win back, and he was forbidden to make any investments, but he had given him a perfunctory role in the company anyway.

"Young master Owen would be well placed to steal funds, perhaps giving money to Mr Phripps to ensure his silence," said Twill, waving his hands to dismiss all assembled.

And so, they examined the company's bookkeeping records, transactions, purchases and wage payments, to find... not a single penny out of place.

"Hmm," said Twill. "This is unexpected. We must check again."

So they did, and eventually Miss Parnacki came to Mr Twill and said "Sir, I have found a discrepancy." He looked at her with hungry glee, until she held up the figures.

"One pound. In the company's favour."

Twill frowned. "That's within our margin of error. Let me see."

Twill now personally checked everything, and Miss Parnacki was correct. A large amount of money was transferred between two of the Dearmans & Son's accounts, but it had grown by one pound during this process and there was no indication why, or of who had done this, only a partially erased word in pencil that said 'MINE'. Twill peered at this carefully.

"Mine? Hmm... Whose?"

At a loss, Mr Twill instructed that the auditors needed to speak to Phripps and the young Owen Dearmans as they were the only two who could have made this transfer, as well as Miss Parsons to see if she could help.

Phripps was extremely tight-lipped about his windfall, just as he had been with his co-workers. He only said that it was for 'petunias', and it was otherwise none of the auditor's business.

Owen Dearmans smiled when they showed him the figures.

"I haven't the foggiest about that sort of thing, as I'm sure Dad will tell you. No head for numbers! I'm clearly putting something into this company though, if we're one pound up."

Miss Parsons was even less helpful, saying that Phripps never told her where the money came from and she didn't really care, although she was aware that the other workers were talking behind their backs and wished he would come clean about whatever it was.

"I know everyone thinks I'm only with him for this money," Miss Parsons said. "But actually, I've admired him for a while. It's just that he always had dirt under his nails, I can't abide a slob. And all he'd ever talk about was his aunt. Then suddenly it wasn't there anymore, and we had a conversation...I know I'm shallow, I'm just a different kind of shallow."

Back at the firm Mr Twill sat in thought, his fingers steepled. Miss Parnacki entered carefully.

"I fear this particular vampire has eluded me." he said dryly.

"Oh no sir, we've got them. And all it took was a stake."

Who does Helen Parnacki suspect of embezzling?

Hint: Investment

87

25. Rare Old Mountain Dew

"A t first I just thought he was **dead drunk,"** said Sandra Mallon about her husband, Peter. "Then I realized he was actually dead."

Detective Inspector Radford nodded solemnly. Sandra had found him splayed in their back garden. Peter had a history of drinking, but the doctor confirmed that it wasn't the alcohol in his system that killed him, but rather the blow to the back of the head.

Constable Axton was doing his usual business of marching around looking under every leaf in the garden, when suddenly he started waving his arms frantically and began pointing at a little metal pot in the distance.

When they got there Radford was surprised. He didn't expect to find a Potcheen still in Chobham. Radford had seen a few of these whenever he visited his mum's home village.

"It's used to make Irish moonshine, incredibly strong, they use grain or potatoes," he told Axton

The smell of burnt peat from the embers confirmed it.

The pot was empty, but Radford would bet that it had been full recently.

"Whose land is this?" he asked Mrs Mallon.

"This is actually on the borders of three people's property."

Classic. You set up your potcheen still on the boundary between lands so that if the police found it, all involved could claim ignorance.

"Who?" Radford asked.

"Liam Walsh, he's the landlord of The Rose of Tralee."

"Irish?"

"Yes, but he plays it up a bit! It helps him with custom. Then there's Arthur Veil, he's an actor, supposedly! And the third is Horace Cleaver, he's one of those people who wants alcohol banned."

"Did they know Peter?"

"Peter was friends with Liam and Arthur. But not Cleaver! He tried handing out pamphlets about prohibition, got bopped on the nose by Peter."

First, they went to the pub. Liam Walsh played up the cheery Irish landlord stereotype as soon as they entered.

"Hello gentlemen, to be sure it's a fine morning to be seeing you in my establishment," he said, beaming.

Once they explained the reason for their presence, he dropped the act.

"Peter dead? Well that's terrible. But I wouldn't know anything about a Potcheen still. I have a license to sell alcohol here, why would I need to be brewing anything illegally?"

"Did you see Peter last night?" Radford said.

"Oh sure, he was here, and he had a few, but he left in fine spirit and with fairly steady legs. I've a few witnesses to that fact!"

They then visited Arthur Veil, sitting in a chair on his front lawn wearing sunglasses despite the overcast weather. He didn't even move until Radford coughed at which point, he jumped.

"Hello?"

Radford introduced himself and Constable Axton, noting that Veil wasn't getting up from the chair.

"Good to see you Inspector, sorry I won't get up, I'm a bit hungover."

Axton picked up an acorn from the ground and lobbed it directly at Veil's head! Veil made no effort to catch it and it hit him squarely on the forehead.

"Ow!"

"He can't see, sir." Axton said.

"You could have just said, Axton!" Radford shouted.

"Temporarily. I hope," Veil said. "It wore off the previous couple of times."

After they broke the news about Peter, Veil said that the still belonged to Liam Walsh. He would brew on stormy days to hide the smoke, keeping an eye on the church's weathervane to ensure that the wind wouldn't blow it toward the local police station. He'd have select friends join him to stoke the fire, bottle the newest batch and drink a bit of the previous one.

"Last night it was me, Liam, Peter and that Cleaver fellow."

"The teetotaller?" Axton said, surprised.

"He's a fiend for it! My eyesight went at some time before midnight, not sure exactly, but Cleaver walked me back to my house. When I left Peter sounded fine, if a bit toasted."

"Didn't he punch Cleaver once?"

Arthur smiled. "The old mountain dew has forged many a new friendship. But also new enmities, sometimes. Peter was teasing Liam about the police seeing the still's smoke last night, since it was such a bright moon. He wasn't taking it in well, if you know what I'm saying. Later the weathervane showed the wind was blowing North-East right toward the station so I did worry what might be happening in my absence! Turns out I was right."

Cleaver was reluctant to even answer the door to them, and when he did his face was a mask of regret.

"I've heard what happened to poor Peter. To my eternal shame I was not just a witness to the sin of drinking alcohol, but an active participant. Curse my weakness!"

"Arthur Veil says you walked him home because he had gone blind?"

"Indeed I did, a small act of kindness which does not make up for my debasement. After that I went home, I felt too ashamed of myself to re-join Liam and Peter... My wife will tell you that."

Back at the pub Liam Walsh admitted being there but said the still belonged to Arthur Veil.

"When I told him about them, he was fascinated, he insisted on building one himself! He's the one who had the argument about the smoke with Peter!"

Walsh said that once Cleaver had taken Arthur Veil off he had also left when the smoke started blowing North-East, but he hadn't been able to convince Peter to leave.

"Well, someone's lying," Radford said to Axton outside the pub.

Axton nodded, then looked surprised. "Wait, you really haven't figured out who yet?"

Who does Constable Axton suspect of killing Peter Mallon?

Hint: Weathervane

90

26. Cold Blood

Joe Hollobone didn't sweat much, which had helped him in the past when he needed to intimidate people but did make it a little harder for him to keep cool when making repairs outside.

What also made it less tolerable was the murdered man. Joe had spent the day getting materials and was delivering them at 6pm, only to find the place crawling with police. Apparently the owner, Tobin Heep, had been found dead by his wife, Jane Heep, about an hour earlier, having left him that morning at 9:30am to go shopping. He had been stabbed with an ice-pick.

"Do you know anyone who would have a grudge against him?" Inspector Knatchbull asked.

"No, Tobin was a kind man!" she cried. "His mother died recently, bequeathed him this antique gold watch, he'd been wearing that and talking about it a lot! Do you think perhaps someone... Oh it's too horrible to contemplate."

"Do you have anyone who could confirm you were out shopping?" Knatchbull asked. Mrs Heep looked horrified.

"You can't possibly think that I... that I would..." she spluttered, tears forming in her eyes. She recovered her composure and answered with effort. "I think a few of the boutiques I went to knew me. But not all of them."

"Did he have any other visitors scheduled today?" asked Knatchbull.

"Just the ice delivery man," Mrs Heep said, and she opened the larder to show a large glistening block of ice. "He was scheduled to come at 4:30."

While the police located the ice-man the building's other tenant arrived. Kurt Weiss, who occupied the basement, was a rather sullen young man who rolled his eyes at Jane Heep's description of her husband.

"Kind? Hah! To his tenants, a miser. Faulty wiring, broken heating! My flat is so cold I feel like it is haunted. And I have no privacy, he lets himself into my place any time he wants to drone on for hours, drinking is bad, gambling is bad. I don't do these things. And now he strides around with his golden watch. He has money to buy that but not to fix my flat?"

"It was a gift from his dead mother," said Knatchbull, unamused. "And Mr Hollobone here is doing some repairs. Where were you today?"

"At my job. I rent deck-chairs at the beach, from 9am. Very busy today, you must understand. People must have seen me do this!"

Knatchbull sent a constable to verify his alibi and then went to question the newly arrived ice delivery man.

"Well well well, Kevin Link," Knatchbull said. "You're an ice delivery man now, are you? Last I checked you preferred things that were hot. Like stolen items."

Kevin Link was a huge beefy looking man with a broken nose and an unhappy expression.

"Listen Mr Knatchbull, I went straight when I got out, I couldn't face going back in again," he mumbled. "Ice is a good gig; we just get the cubes off the boat and deliver them around here. I don't want to lose it."

"You might lose it soon anyway!" Kurt Weiss declared from nearby. "I hear in America they have refrigerator machines that keep things cold with electrics."

Knatchbull got a constable to take Weiss elsewhere and questioned Link about his delivery.

"I was due at 10am, but was delayed, so I delivered the ice late," he said.

"At 4:30?" Knatchbull asked.

"What, no! At 10:30. He was a bit narky about it, saying he'd complain about me, tapping this golden looking watch... Chipped himself off a bit of ice for a cocktail and paid me. Then off I went."

"Mrs Heep says you were due at 4:30," Knatchbull said, looking at the large block of ice in the cupboard.

"I dunno about that. It said 10 on the sheet and I came at 10:30."

Joe had been in his share of meat warehouses and knew how long it usually took ice to melt and considering how hot and sunny the day had been, the ice block seemed a bit larger to him than it should have been. He thought Knatchbull might have noticed this as well.

"Can anyone vouch for that, Kevin?" the inspector asked.

"Not really. It's a one-man job, the delivery. I delivered to a few other people after him, but I don't reckon they remember me. No-one really cares once they have the ice. But why would I do him in anyway? Even if I wasn't straight, you would know I was here."

"You're not one of the world's greatest thinkers, Link," Knatchbull said. "Maybe you just saw the watch and animal instinct took over."

The constable returned to say that Weiss' boss would confirm he was setting up deck chairs all day, even eating his lunch on the beach. It was still quite hot even as the sun was setting and Knatchbull sat down next to the melting ice block. Joe joined him and nodded.

"Well, it's fairly obvious what happened," Joe said.

Who does Joe Hollobone suspect killed Tobin Heep?

27. The Stings

It was halfway through their lunch when Mary Fitzgerald's sister Philomena opened her purse and pulled out a notebook.

"Now, don't get funny about this, Mare," Philomena began. "But I think the old lady next door is being held hostage by anarchists."

"Oh Phil," said Mary, patting her sister's hand. "Remember when you thought the postman was an assassin sent by the King of Spain?"

"I was seven then, Mare..."

"Yes, well last year you thought your manicurist was Mata Hari..."

Philomena pointed accusingly. "You promised when we were little that you would investigate anything I thought was worth looking into, and in exchange I'd always do you a French braid the way you like it!"

Mary sighed, "OK, tell me about the anarchists."

Mary was visiting Philomena at her house in Grosvenor Square in Mayfair, a very high-class area filled with Dukes, Robber Barons, and the occasional disaffected scion.

"OK, so the lady next door, Dame Hillary Finch, she's sometimes a bit standoffish but generally OK for a natter if you catch her in the open, you know what I mean!"

"I do."

"Anyway, one day I saw these two peculiar men hanging around in her back garden. They're both wearing these sorts of workmen's clothes but they didn't look like workmen, they were rather more... smart looking. Anyway, I asked them what they were doing, and they said they were dealing with a wasp's nest! And they sort of pointed at it in the tree."

"OK," said Mary.

"But the next day they were there again, and the next. And the wasp's nest was still there! How long does it take to get rid of a nest? And while they were doing that Dame Hillary was nowhere to be seen!"

"Maybe she went away?" Mary asked.

"She would have told me!" said Philomena. "She loved to boast about her trips, and she was so neurotic about burglars! She's even more vigilant

than I am, she's always going down the
local police station saying so-and-so is
playing jazz records too loud, or the man
next door is burning too much incense.
Ironic really. Anyway, I looked at the
wasp's nest and it looked a bit...papery."

"Wasp's nests do look papery, Phil,"
Mary said.

"I meant fake papery! So I said to them
'you've been here a while' and they were
really cagy, said it's a special kind of
wasp's nest, takes a long time to remove."

"Hmm." Said Mary. "Are they still
there now?"

"Oh yes. Have a squizz." Philomena said, pulling out binoculars.

"Phil!" Mary said, but then went to the back window and peered
through. Just as Philomena said, there were two men hanging around in
the garden next door. Every now and then one of them would go up the
ladder to where the wasp's nest was, then come back down again. Mary
did not see any wasps near the nest or anywhere in the garden.

Mary dropped the binoculars and looked at Philomena. "It is a bit
odd," she admitted.

"I knew it!" Philomena squealed.

"But there is probably a rational explanation. Come on."

Mary went into Philomena's garden and leaned over the fence waving
at the men. As Philomena said they looked at her, not with hostility but
with a mix of exasperation and wariness. From this angle she noted that
they both wore thick, well-polished boots, and had very good posture.

"Can I help you?" One of them asked.

"Hullo, just wondered how the whole wasp's nest situation is going.
Can't see a lot of wasps."

The men looked at each other, then her. "They're all inside," said
one of them.

"Oh, I see, like Dame Hillary. Is she at home?"

"No, she's staying with relatives. Until the nest is gone," said the
other man.

"That's funny, I didn't see her leave," said Philomena, who had now also popped over the fence. "Maybe I should ask Lord Marchant-Whyte on the other side if he saw her leave?"

At that the two men's eyes went briefly wide, but they quickly controlled it and shrugged. "Do what you like, miss. Excuse me."

One of them went very quickly inside the house, letting himself in with what Philomena whispered looked like the Dame's spare keys. The other man remained, putting his hands behind his back and pacing carefully around the garden.

Philomena went back inside. "I only said that about Lord Marchant-Whyte to see if I got a reaction, and boy, did I! But now I'm thinking we should talk to him, maybe he knows something?"

Mary nodded. "It's possible, but I remember you briefly thought he was a south-seas pirate..."

Philomena rolled her eyes. "It was his moustaches, they're enormous and so waxy! And he always had these brightly coloured boxes like treasure chests! Turns out he's just a boring old importer from Bolivia."

As they left Philomena's house, they saw a car draw up and a small fashionable looking woman stepped out of the back.

"Dame Hillary?" Philomena squealed and pelted forward.

"Yes dear, I've just got back from staying with relatives," Dame Hillary said, a little stiffly. "I must go and see how the wasp's nest situation is going."

As she entered her house Philomena ran back into her own followed by Mary, and they watched as Dame Hillary entered her garden and had what looked like a rather stilted conversation with the two men.

"I've changed my mind," Philomena said. "She's not been kidnapped, she's the Queen Anarchist!"

"Actually, Phil dear, I think I know exactly who the men in the Dame's garden are," said Mary.

Who does Mary Fitzgerald think the two men in the garden are?

Hint: *Ladder*

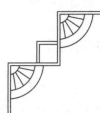

28. Ragpicker's End

Henry Wellbelove had lived in a typical rag and bone man's yard, filled with old broken objects, discarded rubbish, reams of used wool, and broken nails. The only thing different was the presence of Henry Wellbelove himself in the middle of the yard, splayed on the ground with a broken China cup next to his hand.

Locals told Detective Inspector Radford that he was always rather well turned out for someone who traded in rubbish and things people no longer needed. He'd often have clean new clothes as he rode down the streets in his horse and cart collecting trash. A bit strange, thought Radford.

"Actually, I think I know exactly why," said Constable Axton, who after 5 minutes of digging through trash had found a filing cabinet disguised as a toy box. Inside they found file cards with names, money amounts, and secrets.

Henry Wellbelove was the Guildford Blackmailer! The force had been looking for him for decades when the occasional victim would come forward, but they had never been able to track him. He always used to cut out letters from newspapers and never met his victims in person, getting them to drop off money at different places. They'd had several sting attempts but never caught him, and no criminal ever seemed to know him either.

"At least this explains why he knew all the secrets," said Radford. "He was picking through their leftovers. Then one of his targets gets wise and serves him a cup of earl grey with a lump of arsenic. But who?"

Combing through his surprisingly well-kept files, they realized most of his remaining victims had died of natural causes or run out of money. It came down to three people that he was still blackmailing when he died.

"We need to question them without letting on who the Blackmailer was," Radford said to Axton. "Watch them like a hawk, boy: the one who knows who he was will be the one who did it."

Jemima Green ran a haberdasher in Stoughton. Radford and Axton asked to speak to her privately and revealed, delicately, that they knew she was formerly Emma Greenaway of Aberdeen and she had left a husband there five years ago. She crumbled.

"Oh God, I had no choice, he was a monster, if I'd stayed, I'd be dead right now."

"It's alright ma'am, we're not here to prosecute you about that. We're investigating the death of your blackmailer," Radford said, while Axton was unrolling various fabrics.

Jemima Green's face showed a mix of surprise and happiness. "The old miser's dead? I can't believe it. Sorry, it's not right to be so happy about that, is it? Who was he? Wait, you won't say, will you."

She sat down hard in a chair. "Of course, it doesn't matter now does it, you know my secret. And the secrets of many others besides, I shouldn't imagine."

"We tried not to read them if we could avoid it," said Axton, his hand stuck in a roll of purple felt.

"There's a shadow gone from this community though," Mrs Green said. "I remember another lady, I won't say her name, she said she got letters from him 40 years ago about an indiscretion. 40 years. Imagine it."

Aksel Holmboe was a local baker, a Norwegian immigrant, formerly a famous skier in his home country, until an accident that led to a rich heiress falling into a fjord led to him fleeing Norway in disgrace.

As they spoke to him, he efficiently went about his day: preparing dough, collecting flour, burning all of his rubbish, and waste in a furnace, cleaning his shop and putting in a fresh batch of loaves.

"Yes, I got the letter, I simply threw it away," Holmboe

said. "I have made my peace with what happened, I will not pay money to a stranger who spies on me. I wish to live a private life."

"The blackmailer's records show that you paid him?" Radford said.

"You trust the word of a criminal, a monster, over mine?" Holmboe asked, arching his eyebrow. "The fjord was a terrible accident. I have dedicated my life since to hard work, I get up at four in the morning and do not rest until the day is done. This man dedicated his life to the misery and exploitation of others. I do not know who he was, but I would gladly have killed him if I had."

Paul Polder was a former smash and grab man turned legit, with a wife, kids, and a job at an accountancy firm. The instant he opened his front door to see Radford and Axton his face fell, and he escorted them into the front garden.

"This is about them letters, isn't it?" Polder said. "I knew him was lying when he said the money would keep him quiet. It's the oldest trick in the book, take the cash and then dob in your target when they're tapped out."

"Are you 'tapped out'?" Radford asked.

"Well, no. Sort of. We've got another baby coming. I figured the blackmailer knew my missus would notice money missing when we're trying to get food for the new one. When it comes between crossing him or her, I know what I'd choose. So he ratted me out."

"Actually, he's dead," said Axton. "We found your name in his files."

"He's never dead?" Polder said disbelievingly. "I would have heard. I still have contacts, you know. Pull the other one."

As they left the house Radford was scratching his head. "I really don't think any of them knew who he actually was," he said.

"No, one of them did," said Axton. "I know exactly who."

Who does Constable Axton suspect of killing Henry Wellbelove?

Hint: Fire

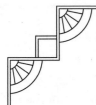

29. The Second Mouse gets the Cheese

Mary was absolutely thrilled to be invited to Routhwick Castle for the weekend. Its owner, the American multi-millionaire Calvin Petty, was well known as a supporter of the arts and renowned for his love of the strange and wonderful, sponsoring artistes from all corners of artistic and bohemian society. The Castle saw a constant turnover of weird and wonderful folk, from bag-pipe playing jazz musicians to narcoleptic Dadaists. It also housed extraordinary works of art from classic to contemporary. She would like to think she was there for her jazz singing, but suspected it was her father's connections instead. However, she was just happy to be going!

She had arrived late at night and after cocktails with a few musicians and other distinguished guests.

"A urinal? In a ballroom? What disgusting madness is this?" said a visiting snob, the Duc de Montpellier.

"That's Marcel Duchamp's 'fountain', man," said an American trumpet player. "It's a readymade, he took an everyday object and made it art by signing it. Not with his own name, obviously."

It was an interesting conversation, but Mary repaired to her room, exhausted by the journey. The next morning, she had come down for breakfast when she heard a commotion in the ballroom.

As she entered, she saw a few of the distinguished guests standing bewildered while the millionaire's butler, Reeves, seemed to be having conniptions.

"The fountain has been stolen!" Reeves shouted, and Mary saw that it was indeed gone, but what stood in its stead was somehow even stranger...

A man lay unconscious in the corner of the room where 'fountain' had been on display. His shabby clothes suggested some kind of robber or vagrant. And between him and them on the floor... were rows of hundreds of inactivated mousetraps!

"Crazy," said the trumpet player, eating a plate of kippers.

"So what happened Reeves, you found this man here and you set up the mousetraps to prevent his escape until the authorities arrive?" said the Duc de Montpellier.

"Not at all!" said Reeves. "If I found an unconscious hooligan, I would lock him in the wine cellar."

"You'd certainly know where that is, Reevesy," said a drawling voice. It was Calvin Petty the second, the host's layabout son. "You've 'borrowed' enough bottles from there recently."

Reeves' cheeks reddened. "I'm the butler, of course I know where the wine cellar is, sir. And if I were to suggest anyone here had a motive for theft it would be someone who had a lot of unpaid gambling debts. Do you know anyone of that description, Master Petty?"

The assembled people muttered amongst themselves excitedly, this was a new form of entertainment for them.

"The answer is simple, we walk to the corner and retrieve this man, wake him up!" said the Duc. "These are mousetraps, not mantraps, it's a simple enough process to cross them with no pain."

"Go ahead, chum," said Petty the second. "But if no-one here will admit to setting them up then I'd be jolly reluctant to walk straight into such a mysterious trap."

The Duc looked more hesitant. "Like what?"

"Not a clue," said Petty II. "Maybe there's poison on the hinges. Maybe the cheese is actually little bombs painted yellow."

"That's ridiculous!" the Duc said.

"As ridiculous as a urinal signed 'R Mutt?'" Petty II said. "In fact, you said last night you found it disgusting. How do we know you didn't try to chuck it out of the window? This poor fellow tries to stop you, you crack him on the head and then set up the mousetraps to keep him from coming after you."

"And where did I get these hundreds of mousetraps?" the Duc said, dismissively.

"Maybe your luggage is full of them. I don't know, I'm not a Duc, am I?"

Mary felt this was getting out of hand.

"Are any mousetraps missing from the kitchen? Or wherever you store them?" She asked Reeves.

"I haven't checked yet... I'll have a look." He spluttered, heading off.

"If anyone had access to them, it'd be Reevesy." Petty II pointed out.

"I think you are just looking to cause trouble, Mr Petty," Mary said. "Does no-one recognize this man?"

Everyone shook their heads.

"It's difficult to tell when he's face down like that," the trumpet player said.

"Is it possible that...Mice were damaging the 'fountain' somehow, and Mr Petty himself had the mousetraps set up, and then the artwork removed, and..."

"And then this gentleman took a huge leap and landed in the middle of them?" the Duc said contemptuously.

He was right. Everything about this was absurd.

"All of the house's mousetraps are gone," said Reeves upon his return. "Or should I say, they are right there. Mr Petty will be furious. Not just about the theft, you understand! But the affront. He has always insisted that every corner of this castle be filled with art at all times. And now that pact has been broken."

"Perhaps," said Mary. "I think I know exactly who this man is."

Who does Mary Fitzgerald think the unconscious man is?

Hint: Readymades

102

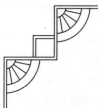

30. London's Burning

Chertsey Fire Station received a call at 2:13am from a man shouting hysterically.

"Oh God, it's all burning, London is an inferno! St Paul's is on fire, the Houses of Parliament are collapsing, it's all ablaze!!"

The fireman who had been woken was briefly shocked, then annoyed.

"Sir, if this is not a prank, I suggest you call the London Fire Brigade and not Chertsey!"

"But I'm in Addlestone!"

The brigade finally arrived at 5am to find that his particular London was a scale model in the garden shed of Meriwether Marville.

The next day Constable Axton surveyed the wreckage

"Wish I'd seen this before the fire!" he said to Detective Inspector Radford, who was questioning Marville.

After his wife's death six years ago Meriweither Marville he had retired early at 56 and then dedicated himself to making a scale model of The City of Westminster area of central London.

"It's actually the area as it was in 1901, when I lived there with Penelope," Marville said. "I used photos and architectural plans but much of it I could build from memory."

"Who knows about it?" DI Radford asked.

"Everyone, I imagine. But no-one has really seen it. I don't allow regular visitors, it's far from complete! I'd only just got the Clock Tower on the Houses of Parliament to work last night. I locked up carefully and went to bed, and then was awoken by the sound of the fire in the shed and when I came down the lock was forced, and my London was burning!"

"The fire brigade couldn't do much," said Axton. "They said it looked like whoever did it knew their onions. They even set it up so that only the model would burn, it wouldn't even spread to the shed!"

"So, who else has seen it?" asked Radford.

"I showed it to that fool Duncan Hamm, he's another model maker. What a mistake that was, now he won't stop bothering me about it!"

"He was jealous?"

"Perhaps, but he wants me to move the whole thing to this model village he's setting up, I told him to get stuffed, but he keeps needling me."

"What about your daughter sir, you said she lives with you?" asked Radford.

"Yes, but she barely remembers the model exists," said Meriwether sourly. "A couple of years ago I showed her, even offered to get her involved, but she couldn't care less. Much more interested in carrying on with that Clegg fellow."

"Gareth Clegg?" said Radford, with interest. Marville nodded, and Radford excused himself and grabbed Axton, knowing their first stop.

Gareth Clegg was a notorious local arsonist, or at least he had been 10 years previously. From churchyards to back gardens nowhere was safe from his crimes. But since his release from prison, he claimed to be entirely reformed, and had in fact taken on a job at one of the farms where he'd previously caused an enormous fire amongst the hay bales.

"I'm surprised the owners trust you," said Radford, finding Clegg clearing out the pig sty.

"Not as surprised as me!" said Clegg. "I only came here to apologize but he offered me the job, said he believed in second chances."

"I believe in facts," said Radford. "Where were you last night?"

"At the pub with a couple of mates. They'll vouch for me. I don't need to set fires anymore, Inspector."

"But you've been courting Millicent Marville?"

Clegg scoffed. "Hardly! She followed me around for a bit, nice girl but too young for me. Asked a few questions about prison, setting fires, I threw her a few bones, but I'd rather talk about farming now. She was just looking for a bit of excitement, I think. Not my department anymore!"

Millicent Marville was at the house when they returned, talking to her father. She was a strong-willed young woman and looked the Inspector straight in the eye.

"No, I have no idea who would do this, but I think it's a blessing. My father was spending all his time in that shed, he needs to get out, get a real life! So much work on these stupid tiny houses, little pigeons in Trafalgar Square, but it's all just toys and play-acting. I remember seeing he had synchronized Big Ben with the actual time! How could he do that and not realize how much of each day he was wasting in there?"

"You've been spending time with Gareth Clegg, I hear," said Radford.

"Oh please Inspector, Gareth's fire-bug days are long gone, he was just a boy. How do we know father didn't just leave a candle burning in there or something? Maybe there were little working gas-lamps for all I know," she said dismissively.

Radford had intended to visit Duncan Hamm but the man himself drove up only minutes later, looking just as distraught as Meriwether.

"Is it true? The whole model? What a waste!" he cried.

"Were you angry that Marville refused to let you put his model in your village?" Radford asked.

"What? No! I have too much respect for Meriwether. And I thought he would come round. Was it an accident?"

"No. Where were you last night, sir?"

"Me? You think I was... Well I was at home with my wife. But sir, I would rather have burned the Mona Lisa! Meriwether is a genius!"

"Shall I arrest him sir?" asked Axton, coming up from behind. "For threatening to burn the Mona Lisa?"

"No, Axton, please pay attention boy."

"Oh, I have sir. I know exactly who did it."

Who does Constable Axton suspect of burning down the London model?

Hint: Clock

31. The Seven Hags

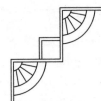

Nestled in a nearby thicket on Warninglid Farm was a group of standing stones, probably from the neolithic era.

"I hope that's not what you want me to repair?" Joe said jokingly to Paul Arnecourt, the farm's owner.

"The Seven Hags?" said Paul. "Found them last winter when I took over the farm, cutting back that thicket. Fancy historian came round, said they're the only standing stones in Sussex."

"But there's only six."

"Bloody hell, you're right. A stone's gone!"

Joe noted a large gouge in the ground where the missing hag must have been. A series of parallel grooves led from there, although the muddy ground made the tracks impossible to follow.

"I'd like to know what blighter thought it was OK to nick one of them!" said Paul. "Sidney, my son, wanted to turn this whole place into a tourist trap. Ridiculous notion, I told him to deal with the slurry pit first, bloody thing seems to be growing. Maybe he thought Six Hags Amusement Park sounded better."

"Who else might have done it?" Asked Joe.

"Well, my old man, Ezekiel, he says he didn't know they were there, but he knows every other stone of this farm like the hairs on his beard! He's been training his two Suffolk Punches for the Heavy Horse ploughing competition ever since he turned the farm over to me, I barely see the old devil. Speaking of old devils, there's Aleister Crowley."

"Crowley? The deviant magician? The wickedest man in the world?"

"That's the one. He's staying in the village right now; says he wants one of the stones to use in his rituals. I should have mentioned that."

The stone could have been taken

Paul's son Sidney was peering at the slurry pit with disgust.

"Tried to help Granddad with the horses but those bigguns never listen to me, I might as well be a flea on their back! So I need to figure out why the slurry's so high."

Joe told him about the missing stone and Sidney gasped.

"A hag's gone? Maybe it just fell over?"

"The stones are too well rooted."

Oh. Well maybe we could get the papers down here! 'Mystery of the vanishing stone!'"

"To bring the tourists in?" said Joe.

"Now hold on, I didn't do it! Putting aside how I'd move it, where would I put it anyway? It's not like I could get it in a cupboard or anything. And the locals are going to go spare. It's got to be Seven Hags, or the tourism aspect is shot!"

Ezekiel Arnecourt was Sidney's father and Paul's grandfather and the former owner of the farm, and was found with his two Suffolk Punch horses, Cain and Abel, ploughing the East field with incredible speed. He stopped when he saw Joe and hopped down.

"It's about them stones, isn't it? I saw you talking to the boy and then the whelp. Never should have uncovered them."

"Sidney said you didn't know they were there."

Ezekiel stroked his wild beard. "I'll be honest, my father told me to steer clear of that area since I was a tyke, said it was the deuce's playground. A doorway to hell. I'm... not a religious man, but I respected my father's teachings. I tried to teach Sidney the same ways, but he was always wilful. And look what happened, as soon as he found the stones that Crowley man cropped up in the village."

"Do you think he took the stone?" Joe asked.

"Maybe. He's welcome to it. If some blackguard needed there to be seven there, maybe six is better."

Joe reluctantly visited Aleister Crowley at the inn in Warninglid village. The sinister seeming self-proclaimed prophet was amused by being questioned by a handyman and expounded for several minutes about occult concepts and druidic rituals.

"Did you take the stone?" Joe asked, interrupting Crowley's comments.

"Ah, now, it would certainly benefit my reputation to say I did, wouldn't it?" said Crowley. "But at the same time, I'm not looking to get arrested. So I'll be honest. I never wanted it in the first place. What was I going to do with a bloody standing stone? It'd be a nice conversation piece but if I'm honest my current lodgings aren't really big enough. I was just looking for publicity, I never thought the thing would actually disappear."

"Did you actually visit the farm?" Joe asked.

"Oh yes, I wanted to see the hags in person. The oldest one chased me off with a shotgun, swearing like a navvy! Although I noticed he was careful not to blaspheme. So, what's it going to be Joe, will you summon the local bobbies and attempt to clap me in irons?"

"Let's just say I know where the seventh Hag is. And why."

Who does Joe Hollobone suspect stole the seventh Hag and why?

32. Who Watches the Watchmakers?

"You're late," said Ralph Messingham, looking at Detective Inspector Radford with thinly concealed distaste.

"We got here as soon as humanly possible, sir," said Radford, noting Messingham's crisply ironed attire and the strange susurration of ticking noises coming from the house behind him. Once he entered the building he saw the source of the ticks: hundreds of clocks, watches, and other time-telling devices adorned the walls.

"I called at 10:17am and it is now 10:53am," Messingham observed, leading them to his drawing room. "If you took the driving route I anticipated, you should have arrived at 10:45am."

"Tempus fugit," said Radford, wishing that Constable Axton had accompanied him this time, but the boy was battling what his mum called "the collywobbles" and wasn't to be disturbed.

In his drawing room sat three other suited men with sour expressions. This was Philip Twice, Peter George, and Darius Vaughn, fellow members of Messingham's horology society, The Worshipful Watchmakers.

They had been enjoying an evening together and were just about to leave when Messingham found that his most valuable possession, a Waltham pocket watch, had been stolen from his dresser, and he immediately demanded the men remain until the police arrived.

"I considered them equally culpable as they all covet it, and they knew where it was as I showed it to them just before we began our dinner at 7:06pm. Then in full sight, I locked it in my dresser and put the key into my jacket pocket."

"We're your friends, Ralph," said Peter George. "I'm sure none of us would steal from you. Maybe you misplaced it?"

"You can use my study for your questioning, Inspector."

Messingham said, ignoring his friend, and DI Radford reasoned that it was as good a place as any.

Philip Twice had known Messingham the longest. "He's really an alright sort once you get past the scowl." He said. "We all had a marvellous venison served by his cook, she left early to give us privacy. We were all together at the table for that, no-one went anywhere. Then we moved into the billiard room, which adjoins his study where the dresser was. We played until about 12 past 9 but I didn't spot anyone sneak into the study. The door was open the entire time and the dresser is in full view, as you can see!"

"Did anyone leave the room at any time?" asked Radford.

"Peter popped outside for a bit to smoke his pipe, about 8:25pm until 8:31pm, we find his tobacco blend a bit strong. He came back in a bit sharpish though, he'd forgotten to put his jacket back on before he went outside, it's rather nippy out there, as I'm sure you've noticed."

"And you had no interest in his watch?"

"Oh, it's extremely interesting, don't get me wrong. But I'm not a thief!"

Peter George, in contrast, was the youngest of the group

and the most in awe of Messingham. "His precision when repairing clocks is incredible! I am fast, but I don't have his delicacy. Surprising that he's such a duffer at billiards. But it's not everyone's game. When he popped off to get brandy at 8:15pm I thought he might be looking to move onto something else but when he came back at 8:20pm he grabbed his cue and went straight back to losing! Darius's just as bad, the blighter owes me 20 quid!"

"Did anyone else go out at any point?" asked Radford.

"Well, I smoked my pipe... and Darius visited the lavatory. 8:08pm to 8:19pm. That counts, right?"

"It does. Were you jealous of Mr Messingham for having the Waltham watch?"

"Of course! But I'm more jealous of his hands. Can't steal those!"

Darius Vaughn was the most annoyed of the three.

"I have several timepieces much more valuable than the Waltham, the cheek of him accusing me. The other two, I don't know about. That Philip Twice is not the gentleman he pretends to be, he started trying to play billiards with his jacket on, ridiculous man. Then he had to go make an urgent phone call at 8:16pm, came back at 8:34pm. Messingham doesn't mind him using his phone apparently. Shame he's not as trusting about his watches!"

"Peter George says you owe him money," said Radford.

Vaughn flushed. "Perhaps I do. Doesn't turn me into a common thief, does it?"

Finally Radford spoke to Messingham again.

"Do you have the truth of it, Inspector? I can't myself think when it could have been done."

Radford was having trouble too. He wished Axton was here, turning over stones and looking behind all the clocks. And then suddenly he saw the answer.

"Actually sir, it's time to make an arrest."

Who does DI Radford suspect of stealing the watch?

Hint: Timing

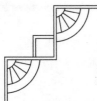

33. Fowl Play

66 **I**'d better get some free eggs out of this,** said Inspector Necessiter as he drove into Dootson Farm.

"I thought they said the problem was they aren't laying?" the constable replied.

"The problem is Bob Dootson is dead on the floor of one of his own hen-houses…"

They were met by Miss Helen Parnacki, the new farm girl.

"I found him this morning," she said meekly, pointing at the hen house. They peered inside, and there was Bob Dootson, flat on his back at the middle of the hen house, the local medical examiner kneeling by him. It was a large wooden shed with a metal floor, with roosting places for 20 chickens along the walls, each occupied by an immobile hen.

"Are they all sleeping?" said Constable Martin.

"They're all dead," said Miss Parnacki.

"Heart attack," said the examiner, standing up with his bag. "Dootson, I mean. Sometime last night, I should think. Was he wearing shoes when you found him?" he asked Miss Parnacki, pointing at the farmer's reddened, calloused feet.

"He always worked barefoot," said Miss Parnacki. "Said he felt closer to the earth."

"I have a friend who's a chiropodist, he'd be fascinated by some of these callouses," the examiner said.

"So not murder, then?" said Inspector Necessiter.

"What about the chickens?" asked Miss Parnacki. "What happened to them?"

"Maybe they all had little heart attacks too. From the surprise?" said Constable Martin.

"Unlikely," said Necessiter.

"Who else is here?"

The farm's only other workers were Bob's wife Harriet and two young men, Donnie Birtwell and Alexander "Sandy" Croshaw. Harriet was in the farmhouse, sitting tearfully in a chair that seemed to be moving side to side strangely with a lot of noise.

"I can't believe it," she sniffed. "He went out last night, said he heard a noise. Then when he didn't come back, I thought... Well, I'll be honest, I thought he'd actually gone to have a couple of drinks over by the tool shed and fallen asleep there."

"What's happening with your chair?" asked Constable Martin.

"Oh, this. It's an idea I had, the side-rocker. It has a little motor in it, rocks you like a baby instead of a regular chair. It's powered by electricity, that's why there's no smoke or anything! All my inventions are powered that way."

"You have others?" said Necessiter.

"Oh yes, the automatic bread-kneader, the curtain closer... Things had been difficult since Bob was worried about money, the hens weren't laying enough, just wandering around pecking at things, the lazy devils! If they'd just stay in their nests. Donnie said they were scared after that fox got in through the floorboards and killed some of them."

"Is that why it has a metal floor?" asked Miss Parnacki.

"Yes, that was my idea, to keep other foxes out. I told Bob if we took my inventions to a patent office, we could make millions, but he would never listen. And now he can't!"

She burst into tears again. Necessiter, Martin, and Parnacki made a discreet exit and went to see Donnie Birtwell. He was feeding the chickens in another hen house.

"It's a real shame, but he brought it on himself," Donnie said, cooing at the hens. "He was always drinking and shouting, sometimes at his wife, sometimes us, sometimes the hens. That was the worst part for me, what did they do wrong?"

"The hens?" said Necessiter, confused.

"Yes! Just because they weren't laying like they should. I was working up the nerve to give him a piece of my mind about that, but it looks like time took care of that for me."

"That sounds a bit threatening to me," said Necessiter, thinking he was unlikely to get any free eggs from this.

"I just care about chickens, Inspector. I need to find out what killed them. I really hope it wasn't fowl paralysis disease."

"Is that a thing?" said Constable Martin, looking queasy.

"We've seen no sign of that in any of the other hens though, Donnie," said Miss Parnacki, and he nodded sagely.

"Where were you last night?" said Necessiter.

"I live in the farmhouse, and I was asleep. It's hard work, farming."
Sandy Cronshaw wasn't at the farm today.

"He's the son of Judge Cronshaw up at the manor, he crashed his bike into one of the fences and his father's making him help out here as a punishment," said Miss Parnacki. "I know where he'll be."

They found him down by the river, fishing. He didn't seem to know that Dootson was dead.

"Really, snuffed it just like that?" he exclaimed. "Does that mean I have to keep helping out? I'll ask Pater I suppose."

"You disliked Bob Dootson?" asked Necessiter.

"Can't say I've given it much thought," said Cronshaw. "It was jolly inconvenient to lose my weekends."

"Where were you last night?" asked Miss Parnacki. "I'm pretty certain you weren't mucking out the cows, like we asked you to do."

"Oh, that. Yes, I was in the pub."

"I get the feeling, young man, that maybe Dootson saw you doing some actual work last night and died of shock," said Necessiter dryly.

"...actually Inspector...," said Miss Parnacki. "I think you might be onto something."

Who does Helen Parnacki suspect killed Bob Dootson and the chickens?

Hint: Invention

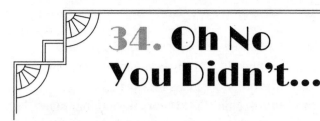

34. Oh No You Didn't...

Mary Fitzgerald never thought she'd be looking into fraud at a
pantomime horse race.

She'd been invited by her friend Harold, a member of The Worshipful
Company of Farriers, London's horse guild, with members from stable
owners to veterinarians. They held an annual charity steeplechase in
Hyde Park where for once the horse owners and carers would be doing
the running. Each pantomime horse comprised two people, the front
and back end, and would have to run a short course with several (very
low) fences to the finish line.

"It began as sort of just a bit of fun," Harold told her as they waited
for the start. "But over the years people have started taking it awfully
seriously. A bit of betting goes on, under the table obviously, and the prize
is a complete meal at Kettner's, wine and everything. So the rules are very
clear, no professional runners or Olympic amateurs, and the people who
register must be the people who run, we even have Gareth McCoy watch
everybody get into the horse costumes. That's him over there!"

Harold pointed at a dignified looking man with a big moustache who
was drinking a glass of Pimm's with the Lord Mayor.

"Aren't they getting dressed now, though?" Mary asked, looking at
her watch.

That was just the beginning of the strangeness. When the pantomime
horses had lined up and the starting pistol was fired, they all ran off at
roughly the same pace, to the amusement and cheers of the crowd, but
halfway through one of the "horses", named Timmerary Tip, suddenly got
a burst of speed, particularly the front half, to such an extent that it raced
ahead of the others and burst through the finish line unopposed, dragging
the back legs across. The crowd were excited but suspicious and their
suspicion grew when the winning horse didn't return and disrobe but kept
running and went round the back of some nearby trees.

The horse's registered occupants were a couple of young stable
hands named Michael Tildrum and Oliver Walker, and when they

emerged from behind the trees they were not greeted by cheers and congratulations but by cries of "cheat!" and some measure of hostility.

After talking with some of the other organisers Harold came to Mary.

"It's a real debacle, Mary! Gareth didn't do his duty because he was jawing with the mayor, so nobody is sure who was in the winning costume, but we all agree there was foul play. I can believe the back half was Tildrum, but whoever was at the front was a trained runner, I'm sure of it."

"Do you have any suspects?" asked Mary.

"Most of the chaps think it was Tom Tildrum, he's Michael's brother, he sprinted in the Olympics in 1928, didn't get anything but still. A few of them think it was Robinson Coy, he's one of the people who run the betting although we've never been able to catch him doing it. Nobody ever catches him, he's good at running away, you see. Personally, I think it might be Kay Bartholomew-Keen, he was at Eton with me, absolute demon on the rugby field, and he was miffed when we banned him last year for tripping another horse."

Mary decided to speak to the suspects. Robinson Coy was first as he was being kept in a tent by one of the heftier stable hands.

"This is false imprisonment!" he shouted as she entered.

"He's free to try and leave and I'm free to stop him," said the stable hand gruffly.

"They think you might have been the front of Timmerary Tip," Mary said.

"Me? That's ridiculous!" he said. "I lost a lot of..."

Then he paused and reconsidered what he was saying.

"... respect, for whoever did that," he finished. "Anyway, I was over by the drinks tent during the race, I'm sure many saw me."

"Don't you take bets on the outcome?" Mary asked.

"Of course not. Maybe me and some of the lads have a chat about who we think might win, but there's no law against that! Have you seen money changing hands? No."

Tom Tildrum was standing with his brother, defending their integrity to a group of officials.

"This is just sour grapes from the other contestants!" he declared. "Michael and Oliver won fair and square! Maybe they got over excited and ran behind the trees, but that is no evidence of cheating!"

"You were in that costume sprinting your life out," said one, poking Tom in the chest.

"Oh please, look at me," said Michael, indicating Tom's now less than athletic form. "He gave it all up after he came 12th in the sprint!"

"Hey!" said Tom, glaring at Michael. "I've still got the talent. But Michael would never let me take the lead in a pantomime horse. He always has to be number one."

"No I don't!" Michael shouted, and the two of them continued squabbling with each other and the judges while Mary went to find Kay Bartholomew-Keen. He was laughing about something with a group of friends and there was one reason why Mary thought him an unlikely suspect: his left leg was in plaster.

"Oh yes, a horse kicked me," he said when he noticed her looking. "Dratted thing."

"Did you see the race?" Mary asked. "What do you think happened there?"

"Blatant cheating," he said dismissively, standing up and shifting his crutch under his left arm. "Last year I was just messing around to make the crowd laugh, but this was obviously an attempt to fix the race."

"Where were you when it happened?" she asked.

Kay grinned. "Am I under interrogation? I'd rather not say, it would be unfair to the parents of a certain young lady," he said, winking.

Mary returned to Harold who was still remonstrating with some judges.

"Harold, it was a fix up. And I know just who was behind this. Or in front of it, I should say."

Who does Mary Fitzgerald suspect was the front end of the winning horse?

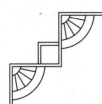

35. Bad Appetite

❝In a way, Gregory's last restaurant review was perhaps his most damning, if only a verbal one. Just before he died he managed to croak out 'bad...', and then he slumped forward, knocking his digestif all over my new blouse!" said his wife Polly, dabbing away a small tear. "At least it might have rinsed off some of the pastry flakes."

And it was bad, for everyone. Gregory Harlow had died at the end of a five-course meal at Che Carousel, the fashionable new French restaurant in Reigate. His two dining guests being his wife Polly, and his best friend and acolyte Quentin Freemont. All three were rushed to hospital but while Gregory went straight to the morgue Polly and Quentin had shown no signs of poisoning.

Detective Inspector Radford had arrived to question the wife and friend as they were ready to be discharged.

Polly and Quentin both professed great upset at Gregory's death, but Radford saw how it could benefit either or both of them: Polly stood to inherit his money, although it was far from a fortune, and Quentin was being "trained" by Gregory to be a critic of the same stature, although after ten years it seemed to be taking a long time. And they both had the opportunity to poison him, seeing as they were sitting at the same table.

"Gregory could be a...difficult man," Polly admitted, sitting in the hospital bed. "But I would never kill him! I've been supporting him for years. Even if I didn't love him, it would be a pretty poor ending to my investment!"

"What about the will?" said Radford.

"I already organize all our finances. Gregory has always been terrible with numbers and words," Polly said, before quickly adding. "Except for the words of his reviews, of course."

Quentin was if anything even more distraught.

"A great light was snuffed out here today. And it's all her fault!" he said, pointing at an oblivious Polly on the other side of the ward.

"You suspect Mrs Harlow?" asked Radford.

"Well, who else?" said Quentin, acidly. "Everyone mocks me for spending ten years at the foot of the master, but she was the one who made it so slow, always blocking us, keeping me from having lessons with him, disinviting me from restaurant visits. I've had to take on a job at the chemists!"

He leaned forward conspiratorially.

And whenever I did join them, I could see she was copying him the whole time, ordering what he'd order, sometimes she'd even have a little notebook, just like his. Maybe she thought she would be his protege! Ridiculous."

"You were there tonight though," said Radford.

"Only because I chanced across Gregory on the street, and he invited me. She controls their entire calendar. I never got a single moment alone with him that night. She never left the table, and I had to miss the entire dessert course because the moules mariniere had given me a bad stomach."

Axton returned with interesting news via the telephone: "'Riche Montmartre', the Head Chef, is really named Robin Martin and is an Australian posing as a Frenchman. No criminal past though, supposedly," said Axton. "Maybe no one wants to eat French food cooked by an Aussie?"

"What if Harlow threatened to expose him?" mused DI Radford to Constable Axton while they headed for the morgue.

"If so, poisoning him at his own restaurant seems like a silly way to avoid scrutiny," said Axton, trying to balance a kidney dish on his elbow.

The medical examiner reported that Harlow had been poisoned with arsenic. Radford had wisely (on Axton's suggestion) submitted the unwashed meal plates for examination as well and the doctor confirmed the presence of arsenic in one of them.

"There are traces of arsenic in the honey on this plate. I think it was baklava," the examiner said. "None on any of the other plates."

This was puzzling. Harlow had been eating the parfait, both Polly and Quentin confirmed this. Chez Carousel's Parfait Royale was its signature dish. The chef would only make one every day, and it was Gregory Harlow's intention to review (and possibly denounce) this famous dessert that had led him to visit the restaurant.

"Could he have had a bite of the baklava?" Radford pondered.

"Never! In his reviews he always said he had to keep the tastes in his mouth 'separate and sacred,'" said Axton. "I was a fan, sir."

They went to see "Riche Montmartre", and after a few minutes of him keeping up his French facade he saw that they knew the truth and slumped down, almost with relief.

"Yeah, I'm Robin Martin. I love France but it's a bit difficult pretending to be French all the time," he said.

"Did you see anyone tamper with the food?" asked Radford.

"No, restaurants are busy work, mate! I keep a close eye on my cooks though, wasn't any of them."

"And do they keep a close eye on you?" asked Axton.

"Why would they need to do that?" said Martin, dryly.

"We thought maybe Harlow knew your secret, threatened to expose you?" said Radford.

"Hardly!" said Martin. "We got on like a Maison flambee. He said we both came from poor backgrounds; he never said a word to me about that, but I felt like he knew. Especially when he said, 'I know what it's like to live with a secret' and gestured to his notebook."

Axton had a thought and pulled a small black notebook from his pocket. "This one? I found it at the scene."

"That's the devil."

Radford took it and opened it to find it...completely blank.

"Well, this explains nothing," he said wearily.

"Actually sir, I think it explains everything," said Axton.

Who does Constable Axton think killed Gregory Harlow?

Hint: Attribution

36. One-Act Tragedy

The murder of Phyllida Montrose was not really a mystery. At 2pm on a sunny Saturday afternoon she was chased into Kensington Gardens by Laurence Chance, the famous poet. In full view of several groups of picnickers and other park occupants he then stabbed her in the stomach with a dagger. He was grabbed by several men but put up no resistance, and a passing doctor declared her dead. When the police arrived on the scene admitted to the crime, he was quite stunned but admitted he had done the crime. There was even a motive: Chance had been reported to have been spending time with Miss Montrose only to be rebuffed for another suitor. A crime of passion from a passionate man with 23 witnesses in broad daylight. And Mary Fitzgerald, to her horror, had been one of them.

So why was Mary investigating it? She knew Phyllida, but they weren't exactly friends. She had jokingly considered murdering her herself a couple of times when she was being particularly cruel or thoughtless. Phyllida had decided being an actress gave her a licence to be dramatic at all times, with no regard for the impact this had on the lives of others. But she obviously didn't deserve to die.

Mary also knew Laurence Chance, and while he hadn't seemed the type to do this, she admitted you could never be sure about these things, especially as there had been rumours of him taking laudanum with Gideon Key, another poet. Laudanum was not known for inducing violence, but the police seemed to think it could have contributed.

And there was one aspect of it all that bothered her, a tiny crack in the perfection: no-one knew where he'd got the dagger. It wasn't his possession, and no-one they had spoken to recognized it.

First she visited Chance in custody, on the grounds of her membership of the entirely fictional 'sisterhood of sobriety', to read him some improving pamphlets.

He was practically catatonic, as she had heard, barely aware of her presence in the room. Drug withdrawal? Some deeper psychosis? How did he manage to confess when he was like this? Maybe he had just nodded his head and they had taken that as assent.

"Did you kill Phyllida?" Mary asked when she knew the policemen outside the cell weren't listening.

He finally managed to look at her, his expression filled with shock, disbelief and regret.

"Yes. I did. I just wanted to know what it was like. To kill."

He looked down, tears forming in his eyes.

"For a poem." He said, his voice barely a whisper.

"Where did you get the dagger?" Mary asked.

He looked angry at this.

"A mean trick." He hissed, and his eyes showed such intensity of hatred that a passing policeman quickly escorted her out of the cell.

Next she decided she should probably speak to Phyllida's friends, such as they were. They mainly comprised the members of the Kensington Theatre Society, a group of aspiring young actors who would stage low budget versions of classic plays in various venues in the area. She found about 5 of them in their usual haunt at the Othello cafe on Brickfield Road, practically revelling in the sensations of shock and horror they felt at her death.

"What a monstrous way to go!" said Kit Bunton, sipping a coffee. "But absolutely in keeping with the rest of her life. Vivid, dramatic, and going to the grave with all her secrets."

"And ours," said Georgia Winterbourne, hitting him with a menu. "This is not a time for jokes, our friend was murdered!"

"Did you know Chance?" Mary asked.

The assembled group nodded.

"He tried to inveigle himself into the group a few weeks back," said Bunton. "I've nothing against poets, we're all brothers under Polyhymnia etc, but he seemed mostly concerned with getting to know Phyllida and she wouldn't have any of it."

Everyone nodded again.

"He said he wanted to write the ultimate sonnet. He was always going on about how he could 'never write about anything unless he experienced it'" said Winterbourne.

"Last year he was doing a poem about being a lumberjack, so he went and did that in Canada apparently, until he got a wicked splinter," said a flighty girl named Emily. "Then he asked to be in one of our plays..."

"She gave him his marching orders, and he couldn't handle it." said Kit. "Filthy drug fiend."

Gideon Key was hiding out at his aunt's house in Bloomsbury but agreed to see Mary in the hope she could argue his case.

"I will admit that Lawrence and I took laudanum," he said, peering through the closed curtains. "I blame Coleridge, he made it seem so bloody glamorous. I had no idea it'd drive him to kill somebody!"

"Do you know where he got the dagger?" she asked.

"Haven't the foggiest. Bob's dagger emporium?"

"Did he ever talk to you about Phyllida?"

"Not really, no! He wasn't the romantic sort really, ironic for a poet! Much more about trying to capture sensations in words: 'What does it feel like to pet a new–born calf, or smell a flower in Italy, etcetera.'"

"He said he wanted to know what it was like to kill," said Mary.

"Well, I imagine he bloody well knows it now! Why couldn't he just pretend? Last year he wanted to know what it was like to be buried in an avalanche, so he got me to stack 20 sacks of potatoes on him in the icehouse. It's a shame he didn't go to Switzerland and do it for real, maybe that poor girl would be alive today."

Mary left Gideon's house and rested her hand on the wall outside, almost stunned by her realisation of the monstrous truth of what had happened in the park that day.

Who does Mary Fitzgerald think is truly responsible for Phyllida's death?

Hint: Simulation

37. The Hermit of Thrunton Wood

Everyone in Lorbottle knew about **Old Harry** in Thrunton Wood. No-one knew where his shack was, but they knew he kept to the Western part of the woods, and did not take kindly to visitors, so nobody went there, and he in turn never left.

Until today, when a passing motorist was shocked by a blood-stained ragged man leaping in front of his car! He exited it only for Old Harry to grab him and desperately croak "I'm the first...", only to collapse on the ground, dead from a gunshot wound to the stomach.

Helen Parnacki noticed that the police had been hesitant to investigate, because the Earl of Northumberland had recently begun having regular shooting parties in the woods.

She had been doing secretarial work at the Earl's house ever since he'd begun entertaining groups of businessmen looking for a taste of the aristocracy. The Earl's estate was low on funds and the visitors had plenty, and he was prepared to be very chummy with them, especially Matthew Arkwright, a copper magnate with low morals but deep pockets. The irony was that the Earl hated guns and really knew nothing about them, preferring bird-watching, but was prepared to pretend just to entertain his 'uncouth' guests.

"I've turned into a school dinner lady!" the Earl's cook would rant to Helen. "Used to just cook for the three of 'em, the two brothers and their sister, now I've got to cook for the Earl and his sister AND do whole banquets for a gang of sniggering oiks!"

The Earl's grounds incorporated the part of the wood where old Harry lived, but the Earl preferred to pretend he didn't exist. This wasn't an option for his gamekeeper Brynwel Jones, who had to deal with Old Harry's poaching.

Nonetheless both men had been smart enough to keep the shooting parties to the Eastern part of the woods, away from the hermit.

But they had been in the woods at the time the examiner said that Old Harry was shot. And she knew for a fact that three of the party members had gone off on their own for various reasons:

The Earl had gone off to chase a rare bird, always more interested in that than actually shooting.

Matthew Arkwright had drunkenly stumbled off to relieve himself in the woods.

And Brynwel Jones had been slipping off to find game for them to shoot.

Inspector Canker arrived at the hall and reluctantly began by questioning the Earl, who seemed nonplussed by the whole situation.

"I don't think it can have been one of my guests," he said to Canker.

"Did anyone hear any other gunshots in the woods?" Canker asked.

"They were all blasting away so regularly close to each other's ears, I doubt they could have heard anything at all," said the Earl frostily.

"Mr Arkwright reportedly apparently slipped off for... a moment, your Grace, and he was in his cups," said Canker, carefully.

"Who told you that?" the Earl said angrily. "I happened to notice that Mr Arkwright's gun was fully loaded when he left and upon his return. So he couldn't have discharged it. And he was only gone for about 20 minutes, so he wouldn't have had time to get anywhere near Old Harry's shack."

"What about the gamekeeper, Mr Jones? Might he have shot Old Harry?"

"I will admit I didn't always know where Jones was," said The Earl. "He does his own thing. He was always telling me he wished I'd let him deal with Old Harry, but murder? I don't think the man has it in him."

Brynwel Jones seemed upset about Old Harry's death and the idea he may have caused it.

"Could he have stolen one of the Earl's guns, topped himself with it?" Canker asked, almost hopefully.

"No, we keep them locked up, nobody has the key except the Earl and me. And Old Harry hated guns, almost as much as the Earl," Jones said.

"Were you very familiar with Old Harry then?" said Canker pointedly.

Helen noticed that Jones began backpedalling immediately. "I mean, obviously not, he never saw anyone! But you can learn a lot about an animal's just from the tracks and broken branches, and Old Harry was the same!"

"You saw him like an animal?" said Canker. "Always poaching from the Earl, causing you problems?"

"No!" said Jones passionately. "His poaching was a pain; I'll give you that. But Old Harry wasn't some mad tramp, I always got a sense he'd had an education, the way he treated the animals in the woods."

"So, you won't mind us having a look at your gun?" said Canker.

Arkwright's attitude to Canker was somehow even more arrogant than the Earl's.

"I have to leave in 30 minutes to catch a train back to Manchester, so let's be quick about this," he said sharply.

"As quick as you were when you slipped off to relieve yourself behind a tree, sir?" said Canker. "How long were you gone, 20 minutes I've heard?"

Arkwright glared at Canker. "Ten minutes. Clearly not enough time to shoot this Old Harold or whoever. And why would I? I have excellent eyesight, I'm not likely to mistake him for a partridge, am I?"

"It has been reported to me that you were somewhat inebriated..."

"That's a long word for you, Inspector," Arkwright snarled. "I didn't fire my gun when I went off. If you can check for that, I suggest you do so."

A constable arrived with news for Canker: Jones' gun had been fired, and the bullets matched that in Old Harry's chest.

"Well, that settles it then," Canker said.

"It certainly does," Helen thought.

Who does Helen Parnacki suspect of killing Old Harry?

Hint: *Relations*

38. Park Royal Rock

Joe tried to avoid being back in London, but Giuseppe Alphonse had hired him when no one else would so when he asked Joe if he would help fix his sweet factory in Park Royal, he went there without a complaint. The factory made Giuseppe's sticks of rock with BRIGHTON all the way through. They were originally made by hand, but an ambitious inventor had given Giuseppe a device that could make the sticks individually with different messages like BLACKPOOL or KISS ME QUICK.

When Joe arrived at the factory, Giuseppe's machine lay idle.

"It's a right bloody palaver Joe!"

Giuseppe showed Joe a stick of rock. At each end it said Brighton. But when Giuseppe broke it in half Joe could see a string of numbers.

"Different numbers in every one!" said Giuseppe "I thought it was an error with the machine, but my usual supplies have been fine. I found these ones last week. Some one has been making them on the sly."

"Who do you suspect?" Joe asked.

"Well, Arthur Moult invented the machine, he's here trying to fix it. Sid Prowse is the night manager; he's over there trying to stay awake. And my sister Maria runs the daytime shift. She's been behaving strangely, started wearing trousers, if you can believe it. You've got to help me Joe, I'm losing money on this and if I don't get the rock in the shops then the candy floss people will wipe me out! Did you know it only takes a pocketful full of sugar to make that stuff?"

Joe went over to where Arthur Moult was tinkering with the enormous device.

"Someone has tinkered with the settings," Moult said without looking at Joe. "I made the interface rather simple so that Mr Alphonse could easily select the message he wanted but someone has accessed the random number generation circuit I installed."

"Why'd you install that, if it was unnecessary?" Joe asked.

Moult now made eye contact with Joe. "I'll be honest Mr Hollobone, my true love is computational machines! But I must put bread on the table, so I jury-rigged one of my own projects into the machine that Mr Alphonse wanted. Everyone here thinks it's a manufacturing device, but it's really a differential analyzer. I wish it could have remained within its true purpose, but at least it's being used."

"So, if it went haywire for some reason then you'd be well placed to remove it and take it back to your laboratory," said Joe.

"Oh, you think I did this deliberately?" Moult said with surprise. "Well, I don't actually need this back, I'm working on a totally new machine with my friend Alan. No, I suggest you think about why someone might need a lot of random numbers to be printed."

Joe was thinking about this when he spoke to the very drowsy looking Mr Prowse.

"Sorry Mr Hollobone, I'm not on top form in the day," Prowse said, yawning, sipping a cup of tea. "Although if I'm honest I'm not on top form in the night either. I had to take the night shift for one reason: bunions."

"You have bunions?" asked Joe, confused.

"No, Mrs Winchester next door does. And Mrs Catchcart. And Shirley down the post office... it's all I bloody hear from my missus when I'm at home, everyone's medical problems, and family secrets. So, for the sake of my marriage, I took a night job and I sleep during the day."

"And you didn't notice the machines making these odd sticks of rock."

Prowse looked round at the contraption.

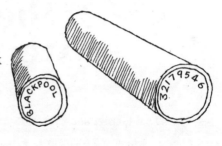

"I don't understand that bloody thing at all. He's lucky he kept all the people who used to roll the rock on as packagers, because otherwise I reckon that analyzer would have been smashed to bits. You don't want to upset the locals."

"Oh yeah, this is Sammy MacTavish's manor, isn't it?" Joe said, casually mentioning a local gangster. "Gambling and..."

"Well, yeah," interrupted Prowse, surprised. "He runs the nightclub up the road in Soho. That's where my wife..."

Then Prowse suddenly slumped forward and began snoring gently.

Joe found Maria hanging around the sugar storage area with her hands in her trouser pockets. When she saw Joe, she whipped around quickly and glared at him.

"Miss Alphonse?"

"You're that bloke my brother uses to fix stuff," she said sharply. "Are you here to fix that machine?"

"Actually, I was trying to find out about these strange sticks of rock. Did you notice who made them?"

"No, but I'll tell you something," she said, moving away from the sugar storage in a cagey way. "Two big jocks turned up this morning saying they was here to collect a shipment of rock, but I didn't know them! Then one of them looked at this paper and we says 'och no, it says PM, not AM' and they scarper."

Joe went to find Giuseppe, who was puzzling over his inventory records.

"Giuseppe, I bet you won't guess who made those sticks of rock."

Who does Joe Hollobone suspect made the sticks of rock?

Hint: Gambling

39. The Zoo Mystery

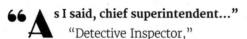

"A s I said, chief superintendent…"

"Detective Inspector," interrupted Detective Inspector Tony Franks.

Trevor Knox paused, then continued: "…if we weren't doing our annual animal audit, these trinkets wouldn't have come to light."

The policeman studied the sapphire encrusted gold brooch.

"A little more than trinkets, sir. This one alone must be worth at least 200 guineas!"

"Yes Miss Parnacki, my temporary assistant, pointed that out. Otherwise I might have consigned them to the bin as junk rather than call you in," said Knox.

Franks looked at Helen Parnacki.

"Are you a bit of an expert, Miss Parnacki?"

"Call me Helen, Inspector. To be honest, any woman would recognize the real thing when she gets this close to it."

"That's a fair comment, I suppose, Helen," said Franks.

The DI looked toward the three other people standing nearby in a grassy space between the gibbon's cage and the mongoose enclosure. Knox introduced them as the three zookeepers who were in charge of the cages where the expensive item had been found.

Gordon McLeish was the head lion keeper and probably the most senior. David Breslaw, as the least experienced, had been looking after the parrots and exotic birds. The third was Phyllis James, who Trevor Knox had described to the policeman as "a bit odd.", but she apparently had a special knack of being able to deal with any creature put into her care.

"Wouldn't normally consider hiring a woman but she got a first in zoology at Cambridge! If she can handle those animals, she can work here," said Knox.

First Franks spoke to Gordon McLeish, who had a rather imperious tone and a mane of golden locks not unlike one of his wards.

"I can't imagine how it could have got in among the lions! The thief would have had to have a death wish," McLeish said with feeling.

Franks looked at him quizzically.

"Surely you are in and out of their cage on a regular basis, Mr McLeish?"

Gordon McLeish was thrown by the implied accusation.

" Well, yes and no... I mean I am, but I know what precautions to take, and I never go in without following the strict safety procedures and accompanied by a back-up keeper."

Suddenly the Inspector heard a strange grunting noise and looked over to see Phyllis James making strange facial expressions at the gibbon shrieking and gurning in the nearby cage.

"A friend of yours, miss?" he said dubiously.

"Yes actually inspector, that's Gary, I'm just telling him that I'm ok." she said with no hint of a smile.

Helen Parnacki watched this exchange between the keeper and the hard-bitten policeman, trying to stifle a chuckle.

"Is that meant to be a joke, madam?" Franks said, but as Phyllis was about to answer more distressed noises came from the mongoose cage.

"If you will excuse me for a moment, Richard needs me."

Miss James moved over to the cage and the mongoose immediately rushed to the bars. Nonplussed, Inspector Franks then turned his attention to the third keeper.

David Breslaw was a wiry, diminutive man, with small features, and as DI Franks spoke to him, he would not make eye contact.

"This was found amongst your cockatoos," the policeman said, dangling a diamond bracelet in front of the keeper."

"Yes sir," said Breslaw, meekly.

"It must be worth two grand of anyone's money!" Franks continued.

"About five and a half I think," said Miss Parnacki, before withdrawing at Franks' hard stare before returning to the avoidant Breslaw.

"Do you know how this stuff was stolen?" Franks said. "Someone slipped into people's houses, unnoticed, like a cat, took what they wanted and slipped out again."

Breslaw remained silent, seemingly petrified by the whole exchange.

"They nicked some very expensive stuff," Franks continued.
"Curiously only one piece was left behind at one property, a ruby and gold snake, which was found mangled on the carpet."

All Breslaw could utter was "Oh."

"Anyway, it was probably someone small and nimble, not unlike yourself," said Franks, leaning forward intimidatingly.

David Breslaw looked very uncomfortable

"I'm not a thief," he suddenly burst out saying. "I just look after animals."

The detective waved the keeper away, "That's all…" then he added "…for now."

Phyllis James returned with a mongoose perched on her shoulder to David Knox's apparent annoyance.

"Miss James, I'm really not sure that creature should be out of its cage?" said Knox.

"Richard is fine with me sir, he needed some contact, he'll always come to me."

"You have an incredible rapport with animals, Phyllis," interjected Miss Parnacki.

"They're happier out of their cages," she insisted. "While Mr Breslaw is happier inside one with them," she added pointedly.

David Knox dismissed all the keepers and Inspector Franks spoke to him.

"Really curious case, this. Someone working here has to be mixed up in it. You've got opinions on everything Miss Parnacki, what do you think?"

"That's your area of expertise officer, I wouldn't dream of treading on your toes," Miss Parnacki replied, modestly.

But she knew exactly who the thief was, and how they did it.

Who did Helen Parnacki suspect of the thefts?

Hint: Snake brooch

40. The Sorrell Sisters

Joe Hollobone's very minor repairs in Philip Kerslaw's office kept being interrupted by Mr Kerslaw's tutting. Normally Joe had no trouble concentrating but it was a very loud, insistent tut that seemed designed to get Joe's attention. Eventually he put the pot of varnish down and turned round.

"Something troubling you, Mr Kerslaw?" Joe asked.

"It is, Mr Hollobone!" said Kerslaw with relief. He spread a dozen pages of paper across his desk and explained.

His firm, Kerslaw and Lake, had been given the duty of executing the will of Mrs Arabella Sorrell. This did not seem a difficult task, as apart from a few personal items, the primary bequest was the ownership of Sorrell Hall in Kent. Furthermore, the testator was a widow and as far as the solicitors knew had only one living relative, her niece, Rebecca Sorrell, who was already the sole resident of the property.

Philip Kerslaw hated to travel due to several medical conditions and so simply sent a letter to Rebecca Sorrell informing her of the situation, assuming that her aunt had probably already told her she would inherit the Hall. Therefore, he was very surprised to receive an irate letter from a Miss Rachel Sorrell.

"At first I thought she was angry that I had gotten her name wrong, but then I read it!"

Joe read the letter, written in tight, regimented lines.

"To Mr Kerslaw,

One was horrified to read your missive demanding that I vacate Sorrell Hall immediately. While my sister might be older than me, my aunt reassured me that I would inherit the property after her death, and I can only imagine that it is the manipulations of my sister that have *led to my name being deliberately removed from the will. As I have no contact with her, despite sharing this house, I can only imagine her reasons for doing so. I thought kidnapping my cat was the depths of her depravity, but..."*

It continued in this vein for several pages of angry, paranoid ranting.

"I was shocked, obviously." Kerslaw said. "I had only just begun drafting a response, reassuring the lady I was unaware of her existence and insisting I wasn't trying to evict her, when I received this letter from a Rosalind Sorrell!"

Joe read this letter too, written with big bold curves.

"Dearest Mr Kerslaw,

One was amused to read that Rebecca is the only niece of dear auntie Arabella, when she wasn't even the favourite niece! I daresay auntie rarely even noticed little Becky padding around the house. I don't mean to suggest I'm the favourite either, auntie was often frustrated when I hung my paintings in the conservatory to dry. That honour falls to Rachel, whose constant bellowing and paranoia matched auntie's demeanour perfectly. Nonetheless as the eldest sister I believe by rights the property should be mine..."

The letter continued in this sardonic manner, with Rosalind asserting that all three sisters lived at the hall but in separate apartments, never coming into contact with each other due to some collective past trauma.

Joe looked at the floorplan of Sorrell Hall. He couldn't see how that was possible, it wasn't exactly a castle, and it had shared dining spaces and bathrooms.

"Of course, just as I was preparing two response letters, I finally received one from the intended recipient, Rebecca..."

Joe picked up and read this letter, which had tiny, quivery handwriting like a mouse with influenza.

"Dear Mr Kerslaw,
One does not want to correct you, as I am sure you have a great deal of experience and must be very skilled to have risen to your position, and I am a simple spinster with no earnings or standing in the community. But I am not the sole Sorrell sister, as I suspect Rachel and Rosalind may have told you. They both despise me for my weakness, and now they think I interfered with the will they hate me even more. I don't know why my Aunt would have done this, but she despised me too, perhaps she simply wished to make the situation worse. I do not even know why Rachel thinks I kidnapped her cat..."

And it went on, with Rebecca heaping ever more scorn on herself.

Kerslaw indicated the other letters on the desk.

"I wrote to them all individually trying to clear it up, but they simply wouldn't listen to reason. Rachel seems convinced the other two intend to kill her, Rosalind seems disinterested in owning the house, but she is the eldest, and poor Rebecca... But then I've never met any of them. For all I know Rebecca is truly a manipulative schemer who has tried to usurp her sister's inheritance."

"Did you witness the will?" asked Joe.

"I did, and Arabella Sorrell may have been a fierce woman, but she was of sound mind. We never discussed why she left it to Rebecca because it was self-evident, she was her only living relative, I thought. Now I have to untangle this web. I'll have to go on the train to Kent and visit this Sorrell Hall, work out which of them actually stands to inherit. It's wet and cold, my sciatica and lumbago will erupt..."

Joe shook his head, "You needn't go. Only one person stands to inherit Sorrell Hall."

Hint: one

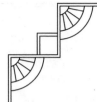

41. The Jazz Advertising Murders

Detective Inspector Ian Dobson peered at the poster. A young woman held a microphone in front of a sunset. "Dorman's English Mustard: Hotter than Jazz on an August night!"

Jazz. He hated it. He wasn't opposed to Yank music; in fact he liked John Philip De Souza. But Jazz was like some kind of madness. And the recent murders proved it:

Giles Markwell, found stabbed wearing black tie and tails on a black and white striped rug in Harrods.

Lucinda Principal, hanged from the neon sign of Sunset Frozen Foods with a hairbrush tied to her hand.

And Paul De Lonnel, discovered in the back room of the Trumpet pub, suffocated by a pile of crumpled up song sheets.

No witnesses, no evidence. But all three victims had worked at the same advertising agency, "Carlton, Smythe, and Broadbent". This new jazz-based advertising campaign was theirs.

Dobson had noticed the posters around London, on buses and tube platforms. Apart from this one there was a tuxedoed man dancing on a huge piano, and a trumpet player surrounded by dancing musical notes.

He'd wanted to go to Soho and roust some musicians, but he was ordered to go to CSB's offices instead. He spoke to Duncan Philips, a "copywriter" who worked with them on the ads.

"Real shame about their deaths, we were going to go national next week, newspaper ads, but the old man has put the kibosh on that. And of course, it's very tragic, etcetera," said Philips.

"Do you listen to jazz? Go to the jazz clubs?" asked Dobson.

"Oh no," said Philips. "Prefer Tchaikovsky. Jazz is just hot right now. Like mustard."

"You've never met any jazz people?" asked Dobson.

"Well, we hired some singer girl to model for the sunset picture. She actually turned up about here 20 minutes before you did. Mary Fitzgerald? She's gabbing with the tea girl."

"A jazz singer?" said Dobson?

"I only met her briefly, De Lonnel did all the art stuff, he was the visualizer, and she was his friend I think. I've no eye for visuals, can't even picture a teapot in my head if you asked me, I just see the word "teapot" in letters."

Dobson made a beeline for the kitchen, but he was intercepted by this Mary Fitzgerald on the way.

"You picked up on the connection, of course? With the posters?" she said quickly.

"Yes of course, all the victims worked on the adverts," he said. "I need to know your whereabouts on the following dates..."

"Oh, I don't have alibis, sorry! What I meant... didn't you notice that..."

As she gabbled on about something, Dobson tried to work out if she was dangerous. She had a posh accent, so she was probably just one of those "bright young things", trying out jazz like she might try on a new coat. He didn't want to step on any official toes but if she was a danger to the public he had to act.

"I imagine you'll be talking to Norman Satner next? Let's go," Fitzgerald said. He had no idea who Norman Satner was, but he wasn't going to let this woman out of his sight, so he followed her as she headed to a building two doors down. The door said "Renton and Knowles".

"Norman Satner's an account executive at R&K, they're CSB's main rivals!" Fitzgerald said as she knocked on the door. "According to Doris, the tea lady, R&K have been trying to poach people from CSB for months!"

Satner was a sweaty fellow bustling around the cramped R&K offices. Everywhere were pinned drawings of all sorts of animals.

"Apologies for the chaos, we're moving to bigger premises soon, we've had an injection of cash," Satner said, drawing a squirrel.

"Is that what you promised the people from CSB, more money?" asked Fitzgerald.

"It's not a crime to offer someone a job!" Satner said "And why would I kill them if I wanted to hire them? They would have come around eventually."

"Maybe if you couldn't have them, nobody could?" said Dobson.

"I'm already too busy trying to come up with this Gentleman's Relish campaign. I don't have time to kill people," said Satner. "I don't really have time to be having this conversation. Once I've found my visual hook for the campaign you can arrest me."

Dobson considered this. Duncan Philips was a cold fish; he could see him offing his co-workers. Mary Fitzgerald looked perfectly nice, but she seemed very determined to prove herself innocent, and she liked jazz. And Norman Satner may have had a reason to resent them, but he was right that he wanted to hire them, not kill them. Who to arrest?

Who do you think committed the "Jazz Advertising Murders"? You probably have a better chance of getting it right than Inspector Dobson does!

Hint: Visuals

138

42. Kind Hearts and Correlations

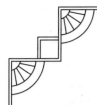

Helen didn't often get a chance to visit her uncle, Ignatius Parnacki, (known as "Paddington" to the press and public but not to his family). His varied police career always made for interesting stories so when he phoned, she knew it must be important.

He was sitting in his preferred chair by the firep as he handed her a file.

"I hope you're not too busy..."

"Working temporary jobs?" she said innocently.

"Of course," he said, giving her a knowing nod. "I'd like your help with an old case."

About 30 years previously a mathematician named Philip Franchester was killed in his house, poisoned. There were three suspects:

His wife Ethel, a maths prodigy restricted by academic sexism.

His colleague Ronald Arbor, famously temperamental.

And his brother David, a mathematician at a different university.

"We put them in our cells while we scoured for evidence, but we were forced to release them all," said her uncle. "Then last week during renovations they found this."

He handed her a piece of paper on which was an unsigned confession saying Philip was a controlling monster, a wild scrawl with a triangle in the corner.

"When they were told they were free to go I imagine they stuffed it into the wall vent. But all of the cells had vents. No way to tell. Handwriting analysis failed. So, footwork is needed. And my feet, well..." he said, tapping one with his cane.

Helen patted his shoulder. "Stay near the phone."

Ethel Franchester was living alone in a nursing home. Her room was packed with doilies and commemorative plates and the ticking of many clocks.

"The other duffers here don't like clocks, reminds them of their time running out," Ethel said frankly. "I love them, mathematically dividing things as we go around and around."

"Does this look familiar?" Helen asked, showing Ethel the confession. Ethel frowned over her glasses.

"Is it to do with Philip? Poor fellow. He was obsessed with timing, everything had to be just so, or I'd get the belt. But I told them all that time ago, I was with my sewing circle when he died."

"You don't recognize the handwriting?" Helen asked.

"It's a bit too wild," Ethel said. "Ronald and David were usually so precise. Think about symbols, young lady."

After this cryptic pronouncement Ethel immediately fell asleep and the nurse ushered Helen out of the room.

Ronald Arbor proved to be difficult to question, because he had died 10 years previously during an illegal bare knuckle boxing match. Helen's uncle made a call to a colleague of his, but when she arrived at the grave, she realised there had been a mix-up and they had in fact exhumed his corpse...

"Been a bit of a problem with the phone-lines," said Sergeant Longton. "Still, there he is."

Helen gazed down at the desiccated body in its checked suit. Her eyes were drawn to the mangled looking hands.

"Is that from the boxing match?" she asked the sergeant.

He peered forward.

"Oh no, damage like that, it takes years of brawling to happen. Take it from me, I'm no stranger to the square ring."

Longton suddenly looked a bit sheepish.

"Not that I've ever been to one of these bare-knuckle affairs," he hastily added. "But by all accounts, this Arbor fellow had many sides. He travelled the four corners of the Earth, numbers and symbols during the day, punches and headbutts in the dark!"

Longton leaned forward conspiratorially.

"In fact, his hands were pretty bashed up when we brought him in years ago," he said quietly. "At first, we thought he'd been in a fight with the victim, but there were no bruises on the body. We questioned him but he insisted he'd never 'squared-up' to Philip but said he should have, and he regretted he'd missed his chance. If only we'd known about this confession."

Helen nodded and took her leave.

After his brother's death, David Franchester had taken holy orders and now lived in a monastery near Sheffield. His room was the opposite of Ethel's, very sparse and spartan but with a few interesting details like a poster of the holy trinity, and a small pyramid.

"I haven't abandoned mathematics. That's impossible," Friar David insisted as he made her some tea. "it's all around us, in the petals of a clover, or the peak of a mountain."

"Did you write this?" Helen asked, showing him the confession. He looked at it carefully.

"My brother was a sick man," he said sadly. "We were such a close group, firing letters back and forth with wild ideas, signed not with names but with symbols. But that passion soured in him, turned to violence. Such a shame"

Helen looked at the papers, then nodded to Brother David. She went to the abbot and asked to use his phone. She shared all the information she'd found with her uncle.

"Well then, I think the solution is clear," he said, and Helen could only agree.

Who do Paddington and Helen Parnacki think killed Philip Franchester?

Hint: Shapes

43. The Three Riddles

66 ●●●A **nd so,** for Cedric Swanson, life was not just for living but for laughing!"

Applause echoed around the grand ballroom at Swanson Hall as the Reverend finished his tribute. Mary Fitzgerald remembered Cedric with great affection, he was both a successful businessman and one of the most entertaining people she knew. His legendary parties were often punctuated by Cedric's clever jokes and puzzles, the bread and butter of his toy business. He loved games, riddles, and pranks, though he didn't like anything too rude, and he was always trying to surprise people.

At the funeral, she thought he might even pop out of the coffin laughing. Afterwards, the family lawyer handed her a note that read:

"Mary, I hope that your tears have now stopped, since I kicked that old bucket with the clogs that I've popped.

There's a big party tonight and I'd like you to attend, firstly to perform before all my close friends. Secondly, I've set riddles for the fruit of my loins, if they solve them my lawyer will give solid gold coins. They'll ask you to help because your mind is keen but please just give hints or you'll ruin my scheme. Good luck, I'll miss you and your singing so sweet.

Your friend, Cedric.

PS: One of the little blighters will cheat!"

At the party, after Mary performed her set to genuine appreciation, she was approached by Dierdre Swanson, Cedric's business-like youngest daughter.

"Miss Fitzgerald, my late father has set me a handwritten riddle to solve. If you assist me in cracking it, I will give you 10% of the value of the sovereign."

"I'm allowed to give you a hint, but I think paying me isn't on."

"A foolish choice, but very well. Here it is. 'My tomato has cucumber my apricot, can you sprout me a radish?'"

Mary pondered it.

"You know, I have no idea on that one. Give me some time to consider it?"

Deirdre smiled tightly.

"Fine. When that crusty old lawyer of my father's got those three pieces of paper out earlier, I knew it would be some nonsense like this. Probably a chocolate coin anyway."

Mary Fitzgerald decided if all the riddles were going to be this tough, she'd need a glass of Veuve Cliquot.

But when she arrived at the buffet table she bumped into George, Cedric's son, who was precariously balancing a plate piled high with food.

"Fantastic set Mary," he said smoothly, sticking out his hand. She shook it and a joy-buzzer briefly vibrated in there. He chuckled.

"Wonder if you could lend an ear to this riddle business?"

"Go on," said Mary, annoyed she hadn't even solved Deidre's yet.

"'I gave you a gift that I came to adore, it belongs to you, but your friends use it more.' I thought maybe it was my bicycle?"

Mary felt that she knew what this one was, thankfully.

"All I can say is, it's something you've had all your life," she said.

George nodded, putting a slice of pie in his mouth. "OK, I'll think about it. When pop told me he was going to do this I thought it would be a funny whiz. How are the girls doing?"

"I'd rather not say," Mary said and decided to try and find Deidre, but she was barely across the dance floor before Charlotte appeared. She had the sharpest mind of the three but seemed sad.

"Hullo Mary. I rather think the old chap had lost his rocker before he went. In his life there wasn't a riddle he came up with I couldn't crack, given time, but this one is nonsense."

"Let me hear it?" asked Mary, unsure she could help.

"All it says is 'Spaghetti, toast and marmalade, steak and kidney pie parade.'"

Mary swore she could hear a chuckle behind her as Charlotte finished.

"I see what you mean. That's quite inscrutable. But maybe he meant for it to take a long time to solve?"

Charlotte considered this.

"Or he's having a good laugh at us beyond the grave."

"I have to say... I think George's might be easier," said Mary, carefully.

"That's actually surprising!" Charlotte said. "Pop always made a big deal out of treating us all equally, despite George being the son. If I'm honest, George loves pranks as much as Pop, so I'm surprised he didn't make George's one tougher!"

"When did you get given the riddles?" Mary asked, thinking.

"Dad's faithful lawyer Stibbons handed them over to us in his office after the funeral. The poor old goat actually nearly had a heart attack when he sat in the chair to retrieve them and there was a whoopee cushion there! Once we'd attended to him, we got the envelopes."

"I see," said Mary. "I think I've solved the most important riddle: What's actually going on!"

What did Mary think was happening and who was behind it?

Hint: Food

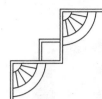

44. We Write In Water

Four hours earlier Helen Parnacki had barely been able to keep pace behind the angry and long striding professor for whom she was currently working as a temporary secretary. Torquil Hardy-Morris, classics fellow at Brasenose College in Oxford, had brought in Helen to help him produce a small but popular literary magazine the college published bimonthly. He had been marching to confront Basil Michaelmas. In the latest issue he had published an article by Michaelmas that claimed William Shakespeare hadn't written his own plays, and that they were actually the work of a little-known writer of the time, Thomas Pope. Hardy-Morris didn't agree with the contentious subject, but he had to admit it sold copies. What he had recently learned, though, was beyond the pale!

The normally mild-mannered Hardy-Morris had burst through the door into Michaelmas's study, where he found the professor casually smoking a cigarette and having a heated discussion with a former student, Richard Malahide. He slammed the door behind him leaving Helen Parnacki but could hear the furious row going on through the closed door.

"Look at these papers, Michaelmas. Your scout O'Hara just showed them to me. Your article was plagiarised from his own work that he sent to you, and you threatened him to keep quiet!"

"Oh Lord… I meant to credit him, I did, but it was such a good article! Surely you understand!" said Michaelmas.

"Can I say something?" another voice interjected, that of Richard Malahide.

"Be quiet Malahide!" both professors shouted at once.

"Mark my words, you will pay dearly for this Michaelmas!" the irate professor shouted, storming out past Helen. They both walked past O'Hara, who looked both vindicated and mortified by the fallout.

True enough, Hardy-Morris immediately went to the Principal and within hours Michaelmas was out on his ear, the end of a long, mostly flawless career (not counting an unproved brief cheating scandal in his youth).

Helen could tell that Hardy-Morris felt this was not enough to repair the damage the scandal would cause his magazine, even if people might appreciate the irony of an article about plagiarizm being itself plagiarized...

Some hours later, Helen and Torquil Hardy-Morris were back in Basil Michaelmas's study, only this time the professor wasn't saying anything, just sitting, slumped in his leather chair over some documents, mouth open, eye's agog, with a Simplo Filler fountain pen protruding from his chest. Also in the room were the scout Henry O'Hara and former student Richard Malahide. "Have you called the police?" said Helen to O'Hara.

"Not yet miss, I didn't know what to do first, Mr Hardy-Morris, was coming towards Mr Michaelmas's room at the same time as me, while this young gentleman was already in here," Richard Malahide quickly interjected "I...I just found him like this!"

Helen Parnacki saw an opportunity to get a few questions in before the police got involved.

"Can I ask what you are doing here Mr Malahide, I heard you were sent down?" she said.

"Yes, caught with your trousers down young sir, literally, and on the master's desk of all places!" said O'Hara quickly.

"That was a misunderstanding, I was drunk, it was my girlfriend, it certainly didn't warrant you and Professor Michaelmas conniving to have me thrown out of Oxford!"

"That still doesn't answer my question," said Helen, cutting in. "What are you doing here Richard?"

Richard Malahide shifted on his feet saying nothing. Professor Hardy-Morris was looking at the papers underneath the dead man.

"Michaelmas must have been looking at his version of the article, here it is." Hardy-Morris pointed out, tapping his finger on a page of typewritten words. "And this is O'Hara's original version." he said, picking up a different type-written page.

"I never meant for this to happen!" piped up O'Hara, his strong Irish brogue coming to the fore.

"Mr Michaelmas and my father were friends in their youth, so it seemed natural that I scout for him. When I first left the document on his desk he told me he thought it had been written by another professor because I'd forgotten to put my name on it! I was so flattered! But when he stole my idea, I had to say something! I never thought he'd do something like this!"

"Come now, nobody kills themself with a pen in the chest. Perhaps his firing wasn't enough for you?" said Hardy-Morris accusingly.

"Well, Malahide gave him that pen as a gift!" said O'Hara, pointing to the other young man. "To try to sway him from pursuing expulsion."

Malahide nodded assent.

"That's right, for all the bloody good it did me. This is the first thing I ever saw him use the pen for! Should have got him a typewriter ribbon," Malahide said gloomily, pointing to the typewriter in the corner. "He's never been off that thing since he got it. Except for when you were using it, O'Hara."

Helen Parnacki looked at them and then Basil Michaelmas's corpse. She knew one of them had murdered Basil. In fact, she'd figured out who and why.

Who did Helen Parnacki suspect had murdered Professor Basil Michaelmas?

Hint: Typewriter

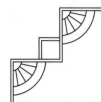

45. Nothing to Mend

When Joe agreed to go to **Wilfred Plumbley's remote farm** and do some repairs while he was away at a cattle auction, he had no idea what it would entail.

Getting to Duncton in West Sussex was a saga of raging gale and freezing rain and a very bumpy taxi ride. It was 4pm and getting dark when he arrived at the imposing Thorneybrook, a huge Tudor mansion.

"Wilfred has done well for himself," thought Joe as he rang the bell.

The door was opened by a smartly dressed middle aged woman who introduced herself as Vera Prentagast, Wilfred's housekeeper and secretary. Vera was friendly and soon had a hot mug of tea in Joe's hand as she took him on a tour of the rambling house.

Joe had been given a list of repairs to various areas of the house, but when he checked the locations and things to be repaired at Thorneybrook, curiously, nothing needed doing. Joe was a little miffed, as he could see his difficult journey had been a waste of time, and his mood was only made worse when Vera informed him that there was no way of getting back to the station as the farm manager had the car and was not due back today.

Joe would have to stay the night, so the housekeeper showed him to a comfortable room and informed him that dinner was at 7.30pm and the occupants of the house always dressed for the occasion.

As he clearly had no dinner jacket, Vera offered to lend him one of the master's as he was roughly the same size as Joe.

At 7.30pm Joe made his way down to the dining room in Wilfred's restrictive dinner jacket where he found three others already seated.

They introduced themselves.

Wilfred's young wife Madeleine was stunningly beautiful, with a strong French accent. His son Trevor had been eight years old last time Joe had seen him but was now in his twenties and surprisingly dapper. The third person was an older woman dressed in black who turned out to be Madeleine's widowed mother, Gertrude Benoit.

The evening was as uncomfortable as the dinner jacket. The son and Wilfred's young wife were not interested in anyone but each other, and the old lady seemed to speak no English, only conversing with her daughter. Joe was wiping crumbs from the dinner jacket when he became aware of something in the pocket, finding an envelope addressed to him. Trying not to draw attention to it he made an excuse and left the room.

Inside the envelope a note read:

"Dear Joe, sorry for the subterfuge, but one of them is trying to kill me. Which?"

Joe realized that the whole trip was so he could help Wilfred find his supposed murderer. He re-entered the dining room looking at the trio with a new perspective.

It was blatantly obvious that Trevor and Madeleine's relationship was more than stepmother and stepson, their flirtatious conversation suggesting a more intimate liaison.

"Your dress is lovely Mrs Plumbley did you buy it in Paris?" said Joe in his most charming voice.

Madeleine was a little surprised by Joe's sudden interest.

"It's Madeleine, Mr Hollowbones," she answered. "Wilfred bought it for me when we were on our honeymoon in Nice."

"If you don't mind... where did you meet Mr Plumbley?" asked Joe.

"I was on a holiday with mama in Monaco, she was recovering from the sudden passing of Monsieur Benoit."

"Your father."

"No, my papa was Bertrand Delacroix."

"I think I've heard of him, a famous writer?"

He noticed that Madame Benoit nodded in response. So she could speak English?

"Didn't he die under mysterious circumstances?" Joe said, innocently. He saw Madame's face purse up at this, as she reflexively fiddled with a number of rings on her left hand. Trevor also gave Joe a sour look, clearly resenting him taking away any of his time with Madeleine.

"I don't know what you're insinuating Joe..." Trevor said acidly "... but Delacroix took his own life so it's a bit of a sensitive subject for Madeleine and her mama."

"Of course, I'm sorry," said Joe. "So Wilfred was in Monaco?"

"That's right, he bumped into Mama on the beach," said Madeleine languidly. "Then she introduced us, and it was l'amour."

Trevor rolled his eyes at this. Madame Benoit's expression, however, was a look of curiosity at Joe, as if only noticing him for the first time.

"So, what are you doing here, Mr Hollobone?" said Trevor, trying to change the subject.

"Your father wanted me to fix things. Is anything broken here you'd like to be fixed, Trevor."

"Maybe my father's..." Trevor started, but then thought better of it and stopped with a look of regret in his eyes.

Vera came to get Joe with news that there was a telephone call from his aunt Winifred. Joe went to answer it, knowing full well it was Wilfred.

"I've been on edge for weeks," said the nervous voice at the other end. "So, who is it?"

Who does Joe Hollobone suspect is trying to kill Wilfred Plumbley?

Hint: Widow

46. Stinging Nettles

Detective Constable Axton had a big beaming smile as he leafed through the latest book in the "Tales of Tippy Tortoise and Barnaby Bluebottle" series.

"I love the bit where Tippy falls into the honey pot, and Poppy the Labrador licks her shell clean Miss! Inspired!"

"Axton, we're not here as book critics," interrupted DI Radford. "We're here to find out who's blackmailing Miss Nettles!"

"Sorry sir, such a big fan." Axton gushed, putting the book down.

"So, Miss Nettles, you thought it was just a petty crime until the letters started arriving?" asked Radford.

"Yes Inspector, most of the items taken were just knick-knacks of very little monetary value," replied Wilhelmina Nettles. "It was only when the first note arrived about two months ago, that I put two and two together and went to look for the drawings."

"This is the first blackmailer's letter?" said Radford, picking up the piece of paper from the table. On it in capital letters read the words "*I WILL SHOW THE CHILDREN EXACTLY WHO YOU REALLY ARE!*"

Radford pondered this. for a moment.

"No demands for money or anything like that?" chipped in Constable Axton.

"No, that came later," replied Miss Nettles. "If the drawings get out it will destroy my legacy as a children's author, officers."

Radford scratched his chin,

"These drawings Miss, are they of a... salacious nature?" he said, awkwardly.

Miss Nettles put her hands on her hips.

"They were drawn by my great friend and mentor, Randolph Tonkington, when I was a hard-up student at Slade school of fine arts in London, many years ago. I would not consider them salacious Inspector, just intimate! However they are quite clearly me and revealing enough to damage my reputation as a children's author I'm afraid."

She had a misty look in her eyes.

"Randolph was a great man. Royal Academy," she added.

Axton was still clutching the book.

"Who else would know about the drawings, like where they were kept and so on?" he asked.

"The only people to visit me here are my older sister Margaret and her husband James...oh and sometimes Brandon Forsythe, he's my publishing agent."

"When was the last time your agent visited you here?" said Radford.

Miss Nettles opened a leather-bound diary on the desk.

"August 7th, about 2 months ago."

She reflected a moment before adding "He drove up from his home in Brighton. I told him that I was thinking of engaging another agent to promote my new series. He wasn't happy, obviously."

"So not Tippy and Barnaby?" interjected Axton.

"No Constable, but I'm afraid it must stay a secret for now."

Axton looked disappointed.

"Sorry, I've been a fan since I was little. My teddy bear was named Tippy."

Radford glared at Axton for this breach of protocol, but Miss Nettles seemed delighted.

"What a nice coincidence!" she said.

She reached for a picture from the shelf of a little girl holding a ragdoll with a smaller child standing next to her. She showed it to Axton.

"This is me with Margaret, Tippy was her doll, I'm not sure she ever approved of me using the name."

"Do you get on with your sister?" asked Radford.

"Well enough I think, she comes and does a little cleaning from time to time, which I pay her for, helps me generally. I don't drive but she does, so I bought a small car, and she drives me locally to places I need to be."

Axton picked up another picture on her desk of a man and a woman.

"Who's this couple?" he asked, as Wilhelmina took the picture from him.

"This is Margaret and her husband James, he has a dentist's practice in Lewes, Purefoy's, in the high street."

"Although whenever I need any minor dental treatment, he's happy to come to the cottage, very attentive, my brother-in-law. He's done the odd house repair too."

"According to the statement you gave to Lewes police, you were at a book signing the day of the burglary. Is that correct Miss?"

Wilhelmina Nettles nodded then elucidated.

"It was at the Library in Lewes, Margaret drove me. I was there for about two hours, then Margaret showed up to take me home. It was after she left that I discovered the robbery,"

Axton looked at the last note she received, it read "*IF YOU WANT THEM BACK YOU WILL PAY, IF YOU DON'T, YOU WILL PAY!*" The postmark was Brighton.

"These were all posted locally then?" Axton asked.

Miss Nettles was sitting at her desk doodling on a sketch pad

"It would appear so Constable, Margaret said that she had heard rumours that there was a gang of Romanies robbing houses around that time. Personally I find gypsies the most romantic of people, I can't imagine they would be up for blackmail?"

Axton agreed, because he knew exactly who had stolen the drawings and who was the blackmailer.

Who does Constable Axton suspect is blackmailing Wilhelmina Nettles?

Hint: Opportunity

Level Two
CASES

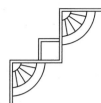

47. The Final Sonata

Eddie Ford, Mary's agent, was doing his best to stay cheery as he told her about all the singing jobs she'd failed to get, but she could sense a deep sadness beneath his disposition.

"What's wrong Eddie? Is it Apollo?"

Ford nodded. "Yes, but not for the reason you might suspect."

Apollo Bardsley, Eddie's biggest client, had recently been found dead in his house, shot in the temple with a smoking gun still clenched in his right hand. The music world was horrified. Bardsley was tempestuous but considered to be one of the greatest violinists in the world.

"Something didn't sit right with me when I heard, Mary, but I'm more convinced than ever, it must have been murder!" Eddie said, toying with a letter opener.

"The gun was in his right hand, but Apollo was left-handed, famously! Everyone knew it, we even promoted him with it, 'the Left-handed Virtuoso.' But he shoots himself with his right hand?"

"Perhaps he wasn't thinking clearly," Mary said.

"If it was instinct he'd be even more likely to use his natural left hand."

"What did the police say?"

"They said it's a clear case of suicide, no need to investigate."

"Did he have any enemies?"

"He acted like he had only enemies. He was rude to everyone, from concert hall owners to waiters. He'd cancel performances at the drop of a hat because the venue was too cold, or the audience would be 'philistines.' He had to protect his legacy and couldn't give a bad performance!"

Eddie sat back in his chair.

"But the people who benefited most from his death were his wife Francesca and his valet Baker. Francesca inherited his money and is free to live life without control, and Baker got a nice stipend and no longer has to hear Apollo shout at him about how his socks aren't correctly ironed. Oh, and there's his brother, Bennett Bardsley, he's a violinist too."

"I've not heard of him."

"Exactly! He's older than Apollo but has been totally outshone. He could easily have a nice little career trading on his brother's fame, but he actively resists it, refuses to play any venues that Apollo played."

"Did you like Apollo?"

Eddie considered this. "He was awful to me. Paranoid and demanding, constantly threatening to get a new agent. Just before he died, he kept going off to secret appointments, I was convinced he was being wooed by another agency. But he was a genius. That's how they are. And it would be a real tragedy if his murderer goes unpunished."

"...Maybe I'll have a look into it."

Eddie looked very relieved. "Would you Mary? It'd take a weight off my mind, maybe I could get you more work!"

Mary found that a little hard to believe but went off anyway.

Her first stop was the Maison Bertaux in Soho, where Francesca Bardsley was being a very merry widow indeed with a crowd of hangers on. She spotted Mary and beckoned her over.

"Fitzgerald!? Come and join the group, we're playing truth or dare!"

Mary sat amongst the crowd and watched as they took it in turns to spill terrible secrets or try to eat a jam doughnut without licking their lips. Eventually it was Francesca's turn, and she chose to do a dare.

"Oh, come Franny, you've done dare the past four times!" said a young man Mary thought was known as Bunny. "We demand some truths."

"I'll tell the truth if little miss Fitzgerald here goes first!" Francesca said daringly. "I hear some very scandalous things about the jazz world."

"OK then, ask me," said Mary.

Francesca asked her a question about that was so rude that she blushed and several of the members of the assembled group covered their ears. Mary could only answer that she had no idea. Then it was her turn to ask Francesca.

"Do you think your husband was murdered?"

This was a shock of a different kind, with several of the people there angrily glaring at Mary for ruining their fun. But Francesca seemed unconcerned and smiled.

"Do you mean because his gun was in his right hand? I've considered it. I was at a doctor's appointment at the time, one of the few things Apollo permitted me to do alone. I was never permitted to go with him to his appointments, of course! But there were many witnesses when I went."

One of the others went to interrupt her but she held up her hand, she wasn't finished.

"I would have liked to have played truth or dare with Apollo. He had a lot of secrets towards the end, secret appointments and meetings, phone conversations I wasn't allowed to hear, cabinets I mustn't open. Even the sound of him playing his damn violin was apparently not permitted for my ears. Just him and Baker."

Francesca picked up a macaron.

"Baker could have done it. Shot him, I mean. Cold eyes, that man. How do you stand a fellow like Apollo for 30 years and not just... snap?"

She crushed it in her hand.

"Now go away. You're boring."

Mary inquired after Arthur Baker and was informed he'd found new employment as a manservant for Hubert Finchley-Green MP. Servants were notoriously tight-lipped about their employers, and she thought it unlikely he'd take kindly to her barging into his new place of work and accusing him of murder in front of a member of parliament, so she deployed her most secret weapon: Her father's valet, Griddle.

Griddle had been extremely kind to her growing up and was one of her few supporters when she had decided to pursue jazz singing instead of the more traditional kind, although he did so in a very stealthy manner, leaving copies of Melody Maker around the place for her father to chance upon. He often sought more excitement than his usual job provided and was a big fan of the books of John Buchan, so when Mary asked him to befriend Arthur Baker at an after-hours club for valets, Griddle was fairly energized.

"Oh, my word! An undercover mission, you say? Do you think I should have a code name? And a disguise? I could fashion a false

moustache from some horsehair..."

"That won't be necessary, dear Griddle. You just need to be your usual friendly self."

Griddle looked somewhat crestfallen. Mary patted his shoulder.

"Of course, you must not indicate for a second that you are associated with me, or the jig will be up!" she added in her best spy voice.

Griddle straightened up immediately. "Yes madam! Subterfuge, that's the watch word! Befriend, extract information, then evacuate the area!"

The next day she waited at her apartment nervously. What if Griddle had gone a bit overboard? Tried to extract the information with hot irons or something? But he arrived smiling, if a little shabbier than usual.

"My word could that fellow drink!" he puffed as he sat in an armchair.

"You'd think he had hollow legs or something. But I got the information for you Miss Fitzgerald. It seems he found Mr Bardsley in his chair with the wound at 2pm, having just returned from taking one of his dinner suits to the menders. He was shocked but he called the police immediately. He found a typewritten note on the side simply explaining that he could not continue and something else that Baker refused to tell me."

"Typewritten? Not handwritten? So, it might not have been written by him?"

Griddle rubbed his head. "I suppose not, although Mr Baker did say his employer had taken to writing everything using his typewriter, he said it was because of the novelty factor. If I'm honest Miss Fitzgerald I'm fairly certain he wasn't telling me everything. When I mentioned how lucky he was to receive the annual payment from Mr Bardsley's estate, he said that was only a recent addition since he found out... then he quickly changed the subject!"

"But he didn't think it could have been murder?"

"No, he scoffed at that. Said no-one would be allowed to take Apollo's life but Apollo himself. He seemed to love the man."

Benjamin Bardsley agreed to meet her quite enthusiastically and she was a bit concerned when she arrived at the restaurant that he viewed her as a possible future conquest. He was a beefy, broad-shouldered fellow with a ruddy complexion, looking rather fit for a 65-year-old.

"Yes, was out of the country when he did it," he said, buttering a piece of toast. "Was climbing Mount Kilimanjaro, breath-taking view. I'm sure my fellow climbers will vouch for me."

"Doesn't it make you sad?" Mary asked.

"A bit, I suppose. You know I was the first violinist in the family? Little runt copied me, couldn't get the hang of it until he started using his left-hand. People love a novelty act, don't they?"

"Were you a bit annoyed he didn't leave you any money?"

"Not at all, I'd have refused it if he had anyway. It's not like I need it, I inherited everything from dear old Papa."

"Because you were the oldest?"

"No, because I'm the biggest. I've got an older brother but he's 5 foot 8 so he got nothing! It was all about strength for Papa, biggest and strongest gets the gold. Spent his life pushing and slapping and occasionally strangling us until the arthritis got too bad. Driving us onto glory."

Benjamin Bardsley suddenly looked rather thoughtful.

"Old geezer didn't really understand real strength. Apollo's reputation casts a bigger shadow than Kilimanjaro. Doubt I'll ever get out of it. Very strong legacy."

Mary managed to escape the restaurant before Bardsley started trying to get her to sit next to him and returned to Eddie Ford's office.

"So, what's the news?" Eddie said, dismissing a young actor and offering Mary a seat.

"Eddie, what was the last concert Apollo played before he died?"

"Let me think... He called off so many... the Albert Hall, three months before, but he stopped halfway in a huff, said someone was talking too loudly. I never heard anything."

"Was it a good performance?"

"Not one of his best, I'll admit, maybe he was distracted."

"I see. Well, I think I know who killed Apollo. But you may not want to hear it. And he wouldn't want you to tell anyone why..."

Who does Mary Fitzgerald think killed Apollo Bardsley, and why would Apollo Bardsley not want the motive to be known?

Hints:
- Apollo Bardsley was hiding something from people, including Francesca.
- Benjamin Bardsley was abroad when the death occurred.
- Apollo was determined to control his own fate.
- Francesca was witnessed at the doctor's.
- Apollo cancelled many concerts for seemingly suspicious reasons.
- Apollo began using a typewriter for any written communications.
- Baker genuinely cared for apollo.
- Baker was entrusted with keeping apollo's secret after his death.
- Apollo's father suffered from a condition which is often hereditary.

48. Dumb Witness

This was going to be Detective Inspector Radford's toughest
assignment yet. He'd never had to solve the murder of a hero before
but here he was, trying to find out who killed Henry Gottle. Gottle
was the greatest of all ventriloquist acts and he practically invented
all of the classic tricks: The drink of water, the
rattling box! He even invented the idea of
the dummy being a cheeky little boy, and
once he'd done it everyone was following
him! As far as Radford was concerned
anyway. When he was a lad, he'd briefly
considered giving up football to join
the ventriloquism academy that Gottle
had briefly taught at, but his parents
wouldn't stump up the cash.

"Look at this, Constable Axton."
he said, pointing at Malcolm, Gottle's
famous dummy, propped in the
corner of the dressing room. "Never
to speak again!"

"It was never speaking in the
first place sir," said Axton, peering
under a chaise longue. "He was
talking while trying not to move his
lips. I saw him once; it wasn't very
impressive. He couldn't pronounce Bs
very well."

Radford had to suppress the desire
to reprimand the Constable right there
on the spot, but he controlled himself
and spoke to the stage manager of the
Palace Pier Theatre, Sherrinford Cook.

"I found him at about 8:50pm, I was about to give him the 10-minute call to climb out of his whiskey glass and get ready to go on. When I went in, he was slumped over, not the first time I've found him like that, but the knife in the stomach was new. Just an ordinary looking knife, probably from the kitchens."

Radford pursed his lips at the stage manager's disrespectful tone. "Who could possibly have wanted to kill him?" he asked.

"Take your pick! Henry was never one to knowingly treat anyone with respect, even as his star was beginning to fade. Charlie Chatsworth, that's 'Cheeky Charlie', hated him, that's for sure, he was supposed to be top of the bill tonight, but Gottle made a call to the Palace Pier's owner and Charlie got bumped down to the warm-up act."

Radford had heard of Cheeky Charlie and didn't reckon him. Of course, he'd be lower billed than Gottle!

"In fact, here he is right now!" Cook exclaimed as Cheeky Charlie stepped into the corridor and froze, suddenly looking like he wanted to immediately reverse his course but knowing he couldn't. He straightened up and held out a hand to Radford.

"Cheeky Charlie's the name, you can't have it, I need it!" he said, the last part being his well-worn catchphrase. Radford neglected to shake his hand and instead flipped over his notebook.

"Charles Chatsworth, Mr Cook here tells me you held a grudge against Mr Gottle."

"Me? NO!" Cheeky Charlie pantomimed extreme shock, although it was hard to tell if he was being insincere or if he was just too used to playing to the back row of the theatre.

"Old Gottle of Geer and I were the best of chums! When I heard he'd lost his gig in the West End I said to him, come on down to Brighton, you can take my slot at the good old Palace Pier for a night or two!"

Radford gave Cook a sidelong glance and Cook shook his head subtly.

"How long was Mr. Chatsworth on stage, Mr Cook?" said Radford.

"He opened the show at 8 and sidled off at 8:30 as planned," said Cook.

Axton appeared Radford, eating a biscuit he'd got from somewhere.

"Witnesses heard Mr Gottle practising in his dressing room at about 8:20..." he said, munching. "...so it seems he must have been killed between then and 8:50."

Radford glared at Cheeky Charlie. "Can you account for your movements between 8:30 and 8:50, Mr Chatsworth?"

Cheeky Charlie looked even sweatier than he already did and glanced at Sherrinford Cook.

"I was having a cigarette out back, as it happens," he said, his smile dropping.

"Did anyone see you?" Radford asked.

"I don't know, probably not. You should be looking at that turban bloke, whatsisname, the Big Amaretti."

"The Great Afanti," said Axton, peering out of the stage door. "Did you pick up your cigarette stubs, Mr Chatsworth?"

"Me? Yeah, always. Um, littering is terrible, don't you agree?" he stammered. "Anyway, I saw Gottle taking the mickey out of this Great Afanti with his dummy, doing the voice and predicting rude things about famous singers, you know 'I foresee that Ging Crosgy will lose the gattle of the garitones, etc etc.' Afanti saw him do it."

Charlie leaned forward confidentially.

"Not to mention he was getting a bit familiar with Afanti's assistant Dora. He kept saying he knew her from somewhere!"

"That's your usual pick-up line, isn't it Chatsworth?" Cook said, flatly. "You were trying it on my wife yesterday."

Charlie leaned forward and muttered to Radford "Listen, can we talk later? In private?"

"Constable, take Mr Chatsworth back to his dressing room, and find this Great Afanti and Dora."

"That won't be a problem sir, they're sharing a dressing room with him." Axton said, taking Cheeky Charlie by the arm.

The Great Afanti looked like every cliche of a mystical fakir Radford had ever seen in films or read in books.

"Inspector, I knew that you would wish to speak with me. It is because of my vision."

"Vision?" Radford asked.

"But of course, the prophetic vision during my alignment with the ancient forces!" Afanti put his fingers either side of his temples and widened his eyes hugely.

Radford shook his head. "No, you're here because..."

"The Great Afanti had a premonition on stage!" Dora exclaimed, by way of explanation. She wore a cross between a belly-dancing outfit and a can-can dancer's dress, her hair arranged in an elaborate golden pile.

"The spirits revealed to him that a death would occur in the theatre, and was that not borne out by the events that followed?" She said.

Radford looked unsure. "Sir, in my experience," he began drily, "People who predict murders tend to be announcing their own intentions."

Afanti looked affronted at this. "I? Commit murder? Sir, when I first pledged myself to the mystical arts in Kathmandu..."

Radford held his hand up. "You can park all this mystical mumbo jumbo for a while, sir. We've already been told that your name is actually Brian Affanberk, and you were born in Birmingham."

Afanti weighed this up, then continued in the same whispery pseudo mystical voice as before.

"My origins are immaterial, Inspector. What is most important is that I regard the golden strand of life to be more precious than any gems or precious metals you might name. I don't doubt you heard that I witnessed Mr Gottle mocking my beliefs. Well, as my dear wife here would attest, I regard those who think my work foolish only prove themselves to be the fool."

Dora nodded, gazing at Afanti with apparent admiration.

"You're married?" Radford asked, looking between the two of them.

"We connected on both a spiritual and a physical level for the first time when the moon..."

"A simple yes will suffice, sir. "

Dora put her hand up to speak, although Radford wasn't sure if she was asking him or Afanti for permission.

"Inspector, my husband could not have committed the crime anyway, he was onstage during the time they think it happened, wasn't he?"

"And what time might that be, Mrs Affanberk?" Radford asked. "I don't remember mentioning it."

She blushed under the thick greasepaint makeup.

"I may have overheard you saying that he must have been murdered between 8:20 and 8:50..."

Radford had already been told by Cook (who was a fountain of gossip) that Dora was known for eavesdropping on people.

In fact, at the time that people had heard Gottle practising in his room she had been seen outside it, spying on some audience members in the auditorium. Most people credited Afanti's 'precognitive abilities' to Dora gathering information from the audience and passing it to her husband.

"The Great Afanti was onstage at that time, so he couldn't have done it anyway!" She said, crossing her arms with finality. "500 witnesses and me by his side the whole time!"

"Not between 8:20 and 8:30, ma'am." Radford pointed out. "Sticking a knife in someone does not take very long, speaking from my own unfortunate experience. Especially if, like your husband, they previously had a side-line in knife-throwing..."

This bit of info he hadn't got from Cook but had in fact been idly noted by Axton, who somehow was able to look at a small torn piece of poster underneath a wooden box in the corridor and work out exactly what used to be written on it.

At the mention of knife-throwing the Great Afanti's face dropped and lost its pseudo mystical expression.

"I...don't do that anymore," he said. "Was it a thrower's knife that killed Henry?"

"That's confidential information." Radford said, although he knew the knife was not that of a knife-thrower but instead a basic kitchen knife. "So where were you just before you went on stage?"

"I was meditating." Afanti said, starting to regather his mystical presence. "In this room. Sharing it with Cheeky Charlie does not allow for many moments of peace."

"If this man meditates then I'm the Dalai Lama," thought Radford.

"Mrs Affanberk, is it true that you and Mr Gottle knew each other?" Radford asked. Dora nodded.

"Yes, we were at school together."

Afanti seemed surprised at this. "You were? But he came from Manchester!"

"Not that school, Brian." Said Dora between clenched teeth, enunciating surprisingly well. Afanti seemed to catch the hint and stopped talking.

Radford was going to inquire further when Axton popped his head round the door.

"Um, sir? The dummy's gone." he said.

"Malcolm's missing?" Radford said with force. "Why the hell wasn't anyone keeping an eye on Gottle's dressing room??"

Radford leapt up and practically ran to Gottle's dressing room, with Axton keeping pace.

"I'm sorry sir, I assumed that since we were both with the main suspects it was unlikely anyone would interfere with the crime scene..."

"Forget the crime scene, Malcolm is a national treasure! Hasn't he suffered enough without being kidnapped?"

"Maybe he got so upset he had to run off and get a drink?" said Axton, immediately regretting his attempt at humour when Radford gave him a cold stare.

In the dressing room the dummy had been propped up against the mirror, and now all that was there was a few black particles. Cook was in there looking genuinely upset for the first time.

"If people think our dressing rooms are unsafe, we'll never be able to book any decent acts. Who would steal that dummy?"

"You don't think they'd be concerned about the murder too?" Asked Axton, tasting one of the black specks.

"No, most people knew what Henry Gottle was like. He even treated his dummy badly, it was a paperweight, a door jamb, sometimes he'd even hit people with it."

Radford had heard enough Gottle-bashing for one day. If Sherrinford Cook hadn't been provided a solid alibi by multiple witnesses over the past two hours he would have arrested him on the spot. But still...

"Listen Cook, I've had it with your..."

"Tea!" said Axton.

"Had it with my tea?" asked Cook, confused.

"These are tea leaves. Left by the, uh, tea-leaf." Axton said. "Where do you make your tea?"

The theatre's kitchen was quite small and inside a young woman with bright red hair and the guiltiest expression Radford had seen was apparently loading a tea urn onto a small cart.

"This is the young lady who heard Mr Gottle practising in his room at 8:20." Axton said. "Miss Dill, I think?"

"O-oh yes sir, I remember thinking he'd really improved on

pronouncing Bs. Anyway sorry, but I've no time to chat, got to get this tea to the customers."

"At 11:40pm?" said Radford, raising an eyebrow.

"It's empty, isn't it? Of water, anyway," Axton said, tapping a dial on the side of the urn.

The young woman went to speak and then just collapsed into tears.

"I'm so sorry! But I had to rescue him!"

She opened the top of the urn to reveal Malcolm the ventriloquist dummy crammed inside.

"I'm Henry's biggest fan! Was his biggest fan..." she said, crying even harder. "What happened to him was terrible, and then I suddenly thought, what if they're after Malcolm too?"

Seeing this girl's apparent mania was a bit of an eye-opener for Radford. What had he been doing idolising Gottle and his puppet? Didn't that make him just as bonkers as her? He had a thought.

"Did any knives go missing from here earlier?" he asked the girl as Axton extracted Malcolm from the urn, pausing to pick a couple of blonde hairs off the dummy.

"You mean the murder weapon? I don't keep count of the knives, sorry! I saw the mystical bloke ripping up a poster someone had put up for a joke about a knife-thrower, then he went to his room, and I heard this weird droning noise like a vacuum sweeper. Maybe he took it? Oh, I'll be fired now won't I! I've thrown this job away!"

"Lots of things are being thrown around here," said Axton "Knives, voices... And yet it seems everyone has an alibi for the time of his murder."

Suddenly Radford held up his hand. Something Axton had said had solved it for him.

"Axton, I know exactly who did this, and why!"

Who does DI Radford suspect killed Henry Gottle?

Hints:
- Gottle sometimes hit people with his dummy.
- The tea girl has red hair.
- Gottle was only heard inside his room at 8:20, not seen.
- Cheeky charlie was very familiar with cook's wife.
- Gottle ran a ventriloquism school.
- Gottle couldn't pronounce his b's.
- Dora affenberk went to school with gottle.
- Apollo's father suffered from a condition which is often hereditary.

49. Happy Families

As Helen Parnacki watched from **behind** the two-way mirror, she reflected that this was really a terrible idea.

Like most women after the war, Helen had been fired from her job when the men came back.

Unlike many women she had returned to work, in many different jobs across the country.

But most people didn't know that Helen's real job was with the British Government. She had been recruited by a supposed Professor of Linguistics named Geraint O'Mordha who had recognised her skills spotting deception and staying under people's radar.

"You're excellent, Helen." Geraint said. "Just what I need. Someone who can go unnoticed."

There was some affection, but she knew she was just a tool to him. Different agents excelled in different environments. He said his other best agent was the loudest, most blustering man you could imagine. But she had exposed several large spy rings and enjoyed the work.

Geraint normally kept her at arm's length for safety's sake, so when he'd asked to meet at Paddington Station Café, she knew it was serious.

"You missed one, Helen. Someone you gave a clean bill of health is in fact a dirty rascal."

"Not Torquil Hardy-Norris? I did warn you about him."

"No, don't be ridiculous." Said Geraint dismissively. "Nobody's recruiting in universities, that's a dead end. We actually don't have a name yet. But it must be one of these three."

Geraint pulled out three Happy Families cards.

Mr. Bun the Baker. That was their code name for Jolyon Tenscott, the supplies manager at Almond Cherry Pies.

Mrs. Pot the Painter. Cynthia Croom, the miserable old dowager who kicked up a fuss over a missing painting.

Mr. Dose The Doctor. Matthias Twill, the embezzler-hating accountant, dedicated to eliminating anyone who would doctor the books.

"You're not suggesting I work for them again?" Helen said. "They'll be too suspicious."

"No, I have a bold endeavour in mind." He said, chuckling.

Geraint's greatest weakness was his love for drama. He wanted the world of espionage to be full of spike-tripped umbrellas and rooms full of poisonous gas, not humdrum surveillance and paperwork.

"I've invited them for a reception with the Prince of Wales," he said.

"Edward??" said Helen. "You're kidding."

"A mere ruse. When they arrive in London, I'll put them in one of our safe houses. I'll excuse myself and in the adjoining room have a loud phone conversation with one of the Prince's lackeys, in which I'll accidentally drop a piece of classified information. You'll scrutinise their reactions."

"How am I supposed to examine them when they'll all know me?"

"You'll be behind the two-way mirror."

"No!" said Helen with disbelief.

"My old boss had it installed when he was convinced there was a mole in the department, but never got to use it. This safe house has all sorts of little tricks. Perfect for our purposes."

"I won't be able to tell who it is simply from their faces." Helen said plainly.

"You have the easy job; I have to get them all to the safe house!" he said. "'Mrs Pot' is as slow as a drugged tortoise."

Helen shook her head. "This plan could expose us both, to no benefit. What if there's more than one?"

"It's definitely just one of them, trust me." Geraint said seriously. "And I'm afraid you've no choice. My higher-ups suspect you as well. It's their neck or yours, 'Miss Bobby the Policeman's Niece'."

Helen didn't like the sound of that.

Geraint gave her the address, somewhere in Wapping. He gave her a key and told her to enter round the back at 8pm that night.

Hours later she carefully approached the location, an innocuous town house. Entering through the backdoor with the key, she had found the surveillance room, a small dusty annex where the two-way mirror looked into a better-appointed reception room.

Sitting inside were the Baker, Painter and Doctor, a full house. Jolyon Tenscott was casually splayed on the sofa shouting small talk at Mr Twill, whose bony frame sat tensely as he scrutinised Tenscott to see if he was an embezzler.

"So you're a bean counter are you, Twill? Bloody boring, I should imagine!" Tenscott bellowed.

"On the contrary." Twill said, his lips pressed together thinly.

In the corner sat Mrs Croom, glaring at the two men with evident hatred, gripping her cane with white knuckles while Geraint hovered by her elbow.

"Mr Smith, if I had known these two... gentlemen would be accompanying me during my audience with the Prince, I would not have come." She hissed in a stage whisper to Geraint, clearly audible by all in the room.

"Terribly sorry madam." Geraint said obsequiously. "The Prince's time is so valuable, and you understand the need for secrecy, of course."

Tenscott lifted his huge bulk with surprising swiftness and then crashed down next to Miss Croom giving her a friendly wink.

"Hullo, Jolyon Tenscott's the name!" He blared. "That's a jolly nice walking stick, is that a Belgian leClercq?"

She just stared at him with undisguised contempt.

The telephone in the adjoining study began ringing, and Geraint gave Helen a surreptitious wink through the mirror and made his way to it. Helen's view of the study was only partial, but she saw Geraint sit down at the desk and pick up the handset.

"Yes? Oh hello Sydney!" Geraint said loudly. "What? Taken ill?" he continued, while fiddling with one of the desk drawers, perhaps to get a pen.

Helen looked at the three suspects, who were all displaying different versions of displeasure. Twill rolled his eyes as if he had expected it, Mrs Croom's lips pursed up like she had eaten a whole basket of lemons, and Tenscott looked almost alarmed at this development.

Something about this was all wrong. This was an unworkable way to spot a spy. And why hadn't Geraint asked another agent to join her behind the mirror?

"Of course I understand. Moving funds from Canada. I sometimes have to move funds around myself!" Geraint continued loudly, still fiddling with the drawer.

Suddenly all the lights went out. Helen pushed her face up to the glass, but she couldn't see a thing. She heard the people in the room crying out in annoyance or confusion, then a strange hissing noise. She heard a sharp crack like a gunshot, followed by a gurgling noise, and then the sound of sudden movement.

The hissing noise stopped and just as suddenly the lights came back on again! The people in the room gasped and from her vantage point Helen could see that Geraint was slumped across the desk, blood pouring from his neck, apparently dead.

Tenscott stood near the desk, looking at the body with horror.

"What the hell happened?" He shouted.

Mrs Croom was sitting in the same spot. Her eyes were darting back and forth between the two men, and she clutched her walking stick even tighter. Was it upside down?

Mr Twill was standing by the lamp and staring at Geraint's body with what almost looked like relief.

Helen knew she couldn't remain behind the mirror. While it would protect her anonymity, the possible fallout of them remaining unaccompanied would be much worse. She left the room and found the hidden door that would lead her into the kitchen area, and then entered the room quickly, speaking before any of them had a chance.

"Mr Smith?" She said, pretending to see his body for the first time. "Dear God!"

She rushed over to him. He was definitely dead. She could see a hole in his throat, like a bullet wound. That would explain the gunshot sound and the gurgling. But what was the hissing noise? And who turned off the lights?

Tenscott was staring at her wagging his finger thoughtfully.

"It's Miss... Parcheesi, isn't it? What a funny coincidence!" He shouted. "She used to work for me, you know.

"A very unlikely coincidence." Said Mr Twill, gliding into the room. "She was previously in my employ as well."

Helen glanced at Mrs Croom to see if she would disclose their connection too but the old woman either didn't recognise her or was choosing not to reveal it yet.

Helen looked at the sight line from the receiving room to the study. It was possible to shoot someone from there. Any of them could have done it. But where was the gun? She needed to keep behaving as if she was a simple secretary.

"I'd better call the police." She said, grabbing for the phone. Tenscott, however, reached his hand out to stop her and Mrs Croom screeched 'STOP!'

Croom stood up dramatically. "Stop right there you silly girl, how do you know it wasn't the phone that killed him??"

Both Tenscott and Twill gave Croom a look of disbelief.

"How, exactly?" Said Twill.

"Perhaps the handset was hooked up to a hidden pistol." Mrs Croom declared. "Hidden in a book or a painting."

"You read too many crime novels." Twill said. "It's not practical to conceal a pistol in an object."

"You are wrong." She said with a sneer, holding tight to her walking stick. "Mr Tenscott agrees with me." She said, pointing to his hand restraining Helen's.

"Not at all madam" said Tenscott, releasing Helen. "I thought the police would think the phone was evidence. Is there another phone here, miss?".

Helen had no idea. "I'm

unfamiliar with this building, Mr Smith just asked me to meet you all here..." she said shyly.

"Spare us the routine." Said Mr Twill. "It's clear what's really going on here."

Had Parnacki deduced the truth?

"Mr Smith was obviously a police inspector, and we are all under suspicion for some crime." Twill said accusingly. "They lured us here for questioning. I'm relieved the masquerade is over, even if it's via this awful act."

"I am not a criminal!" Said Mrs Croom loudly.

"Didn't I see your name in the papers regarding a stolen painting?" said Tenscott, scratching his head.

"I was the victim, not the perpetrator!" Croom shrieked. "Those terrible events have forced me to take steps to ensure I can defend myself at all times, which is also not a crime!"

As they squabbled Helen was scanning the room for any evidence of a gun. It could have been quickly hidden in the bookcase, but there was no sign of any disturbance. None of the suspects showed any sign of suspicious bulges in their clothing, thank goodness. The room's door was strangely reinforced with a rubber seal around the edges, but nothing was concealed in it.

Helen moved over to the lamp where Twill had been standing. No sign of a gun, but she saw a small switch hidden just behind the table. Twill walked over to her.

"Yes, a hidden light switch," he said. "I noticed it earlier and when the lights went out, I used it to turn them back on."

Mrs Croom scoffed. "More likely you used it to turn them off in the first place!"

Twill shook his head. "The most likely suspect for the shooting is clearly Mr Tenscott. He was standing closest to Mr Smith when he was shot."

"Preposterous!" shouted Tenscott. "I merely rushed forward when I heard the shot."

"Yes, you do seem to be able to move faster than you would think for a man of your girth." said Twill thoughtfully.

"I think you could both be confederates." said Croom, glaring at

Tenscott. "One on the lights, one with the... weapon." She gripped her cane even tighter at this.

Tenscott turned to look at Helen, his normally ingenuous expression suddenly becoming darker.

"I think the most likely suspect is actually Miss Parnacki." He said. "The room goes dark, this man is shot, and then she suddenly appears from nowhere. We have only her word that she works with Mr 'Smith'. Do you have any proof of that, my dear?"

Geraint hadn't provided her with any false identification documents for this. Her only thought was what might be in the drawer he was fiddling with.

"Hold on a second." She said, reaching for the desk. Tenscott looked alarmed again, but she beckoned him round so he could watch and ensure she wasn't grabbing a gun or anything. She pulled open the drawer to find only a few broken pencils. However, as they looked closer, she could see what looked like a small handle, like a knob or a lever, and next to that some kind of switch. She turned the handle and heard that strange hissing noise coming from the receiving room again. Tenscott very quickly pushed the handle back to its original position and the hissing stopped.

"Do you know what that does?" he asked.

"I didn't, but I think I do now." Helen said, suddenly understanding. "And I know who shot Geraint, and why."

And she also knew who the spy was.

Who does Helen Parnacki suspect of shooting Geraint O'Mordha and of being the spy?

Hints:
- The plan is not a good way of spotting a spy.
- Geraint was fiddling with something when the lights went out.
- Mrs Groom seems convinced pistols can be hidden in objects.
- The hissing sound ended after Geraint was shot.
- The office door is strangely reinforced with a rubber seal.
- Geraint's killer and the spy may not be the same person.

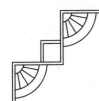

50. Gwendolyn

On any other day, if you'd asked Detective Inspector Radford if dead people could have an expression, he'd say no. Once the brain switches off, the face usually just goes slack. But tonight, he couldn't help but see fixed on Oswald Piper's face a sort of shocked betrayal.

Radford and Axton had arrived at the Piper estate at 1am with the medical examiner in tow.

Small but stylish, the mansion sat in the middle of the more salubrious part of Staines.

They were greeted at the door by Percival Catcher, Piper's personal valet, a thin, goggle eyed man looking rather pale. He didn't lead them to where Piper's body was supposedly laying, but instead to the living room where Piper's wife, Katherine, sat in a chair in the lounge casually drinking a glass of whiskey. Next to her, looking bleary eyed and annoyed in a dressing gown, sat their only houseguest, Mark Swan. They both looked up at the policemen with interest.

"I suggest Ma'am show you the body, sirs, as the safe has been robbed and she knows more about its contents than I do." Catcher said quietly.

"Oh yes, the squeamishness. Fine," Katherine Piper said, handing her empty glass to him. She stood quickly and led them down a short cramped corridor to Oswald's study, small but rather well kept, with a large brass safe in the corner. The safe stood open, with no signs of damage. Oswald Piper lay on his back in front of it in a pool of blood, a single spot of blood on his chest and that look of betrayal on his face. Axton went over to the window, which had been smashed and opened.

"I was awoken by the sound of a gunshot at about 10 past 12," she said, "I rushed to the office and found Oswald like this, and the safe was open. He had a lot of money in there...ten thousand pounds I think he said... and my Gwendolyn."

Radford was confused. "Gwendolyn?"

Katherine Piper smiled shyly. "My...childhood doll. She's very precious to me, so I asked Oswald if I could keep her in there.

Whenever my niece and nephew come round I can see the little beasts want to get their sticky fingers on her, so we locked her away in his safe. Didn't anticipate that some bloody thief would decide to steal everything inside. Where do you think she might be? Are there any clues?"

Radford indicated that Axton should take her out of the room while the medical examiner worked.

"It was the gunshot that did it, sure enough," he said, standing up. "Point blank to the chest, I would imagine, a small pistol."

"Maybe he caught the robber in the act and got a bullet for his troubles." Radford said to the examiner. "There's no way he could have shot him and then opened the safe even if he had the combination, because Mrs Piper must have been in here in about 30 seconds."

"If her story can be believed," said the examiner.

"Well, obviously," Radford said.

"There's also blood inside the safe," said Axton from the doorway.

"Constable, will you please begin searching this house for the money and the...doll," said Radford, and Axton saluted and disappeared.

By Radford's reckoning, Katherine was the most likely suspect: the wife always was. But the supposedly squeamish valet and the houseguest could also have done it.

It definitely wasn't a burglar, though. Radford didn't pick up on details in the same way Axton did, but he knew for a fact that if you broke a window to get into a house, there would at least be some glass on the carpet...

Radford decided to talk to Mark Swan first as he was the outsider in this household. He seemed very upset by the death of his friend.

"I know Oswald through the Architectural Society. We had a nice evening, we all went out to the opera, actually. Oswald paid, he's a very generous man. We came back here for a drink and he offered me his spare room, very kind to him. Then at about, I don't know, midnight, I'm woken by this loud noise, like a gun, so I spring up and charge through the house and I find his wife, Katharine, standing over his body looking miserable."

"She was already there?" Radford asked. "You didn't bump into her in the corridor or something?"

"No...but their bedroom is closer to his study, it does make sense," said Swan. "Then Catcher came up behind me, but he took one look at the body and ran away! I think I heard him being sick in their downstairs lavatory."

"Yes, Mrs Piper said he was squeamish. But the blood didn't bother you?"

"Of course it bothered me!" Swan said angrily. "My best friend has been murdered!"

"Were you aware that he had a safe full of money on the premises?" asked Radford pointedly.

"I never talked about money with Oswald, that wasn't important to either of us."

"Have you had any money issues recently?"

Swan paused. "I... I have been convinced to make some unwise investments. But I didn't kill Oswald! I couldn't even have been in the room when the shot happened, I arrived afterwards!"

"I'm not saying you did it, sir, but there may well be alternative entrances and exits to the room. The broken window, for example."

"Well, exactly!" Swan said in exasperation. "Why are you interrogating us when you should be looking for a burglar of some kind?"

"I'm just trying to establish some facts, sir," said Radford drily.

"Yes, of course," said Swan, calming visibly.

"Were Katharine and Oswald a happy couple?"

"They seemed so," Swan said, rubbing his chin. "They married about 2 years ago, she's very charming apart from all that..." he looked around to see if she was within earshot. "...Gwendolyn nonsense," he finished, a bitter expression on his face.

"And he cared for her?"

"Oh yes, he doted like mad. He always used to tell her that he would do anything for her. Keeping a doll in an safe is a good example of that."

"And how does she feel about you?"

Swan wagged a finger in Radford's face.

"There's no funny business, if that's what you're implying. She's happy to chat to me but I have more of a rapport with Catcher than her!"

Radford decided to speak to Catcher next. Oswald Piper's valet was wandering around in the kitchen with a stunned look on his face.

"I don't know what to do, sir." He said quietly. "I've worked for Mr Piper almost my entire life. I do the cleaning, sometimes even the cooking when Mrs Pool isn't here. I was a young member of the staff at his parent's estate, and when he left it made sense that I go with him. He wasn't always an easy man to live with, but he was always fair."

"I can tell seeing his body upset you," said Radford, helping Catcher tidy up some cups.

"It did, but it's not just that, I have a... condition, I faint at the sight of blood. I was originally intended by my family to be a doctor like my father, but after my first collapse at medical school the old man disowned me. I couldn't even go to fight in the war like my beloved brother. He's a doctor now. Though I suspect he killed more men in the war than he saved."

"What about Mrs Piper? Will she keep you on?"

Catcher considered this. "I can't rightly say. She's a very nice lady, Mrs Piper, she's never been cruel or unpleasant. But I don't think she sees me as a person. That's not unusual in service, I know, but usually even when they're ignoring the help you can sense they know they're there. But to Mrs Piper, I think I'm something like a tea trolley."

"Did you know about Mr Piper's safe?" asked Radford.

"Oh yes, he was very proud of it, if I'm honest I think he just liked to have it as a kind of decoration."

"And to store the money."

Catcher scratched his head. "I have to say, I never heard him mention any money. Of course the master was under no obligation to share all the details of his financial affairs with me, but he usually did, I daresay I knew how much everything he bought cost, he was a frugal man."

"What about the doll?"

Catcher raised his eyebrows. "Gwendolyn? Yes, madam was most agitated by the possibility that mistress Georgina and master Liam would steal her doll, so the master consented to put her in the safe. I think he was actually quite happy to have something to put inside it! Unless I'm wrong about the money."

"Do you know the combination?" asked Radford.

"I..." began Catcher, when suddenly the both of them were jolted by a loud thumping noise coming from above them. They looked up in alarm, only to hear a muffled 'Sorry!' from the floor above.

"I believe your constable may have fallen off the armoire," Catcher said dryly.

"The combination?" said Radford, unable to be distracted.

"He never told me. I don't believe he even told madam; it was his little secret. But he was not a subtle man, always whistling the 1812 overture. I never tried to open it; I should add."

A slightly ruffled looking Constable Axton came into the kitchen, his arms covered in soot.

"No luck on the money or Gwendolyn, sir. I thought I found her briefly, but it was a teddy bear someone had stuffed up a chimney."

He tried to hand it to Radford who pointed at the kitchen counter instead.

"That would be Master Liam's work I suspect," said Catcher. "You can see why madam may have feared for her doll."

Axton marched off again shouting something about going on the roof, but before Radford could stop him Katharine Piper appeared in front of him.

"Inspector! Have you found Gwendolyn?"

Radford stepped back.

"Not yet madam, we're still establishing what has happened."

"So nothing from any patrol cars?" She said, with apparent seriousness. "You haven't put out an APB?"

"I think you might be listening to too many radio dramas, ma'am. We're concentrating on things here first before we put out any... bulletins."

She sat down, dissatisfied.

"When did your husband tell you he was storing ten thousand pounds in the safe?" Radford asked.

"Last week I think he withdrew his savings from the bank because he was worried there would be another crash."

She thought for a moment.

"Except maybe that was a lie. Because he never mentioned savings before. Perhaps he never went to the bank," she added. "It's a lot of money!"

"It is indeed." said Radford thoughtfully. "Did anyone ever show any interest in your husband's safe? Or, um, your doll."

"Not outwardly, but he told literally everyone about the safe. And Gwendolyn, well, she only has sentimental value, Inspector. She's not some rare collector's edition keepsake. But she's been with me since the beginning. Do please try to find her!"

Suddenly Axton appeared in the room with a big beaming smile on his face and presented a rather ragged, worn cotton doll with a painted porcelain face to Katharine Piper.

"Is this Gwendolyn?" he asked.

She responded by swiping the doll from his

hands and pressing it against her face before cuddling it in her arms, her expression one of complete contentment.

"It was under the valet's bed sir," Axton said to the visible alarm of Catcher. "I also found this."

He pulled an object wrapped in a handkerchief out of his pocket and opened it with a pen to reveal a Luger, the favoured pistol of German soldiers in WW1. Radford sniffed the barrel. Recently fired.

"I... I didn't do it!" Catcher said. "My brother sent that to me years ago, one of his war trophies, a sign of his contempt. But I've never used it!"

Radford looked at Mrs Piper, Catcher and Swan, then finally at Axton. He felt the pieces coming together. If what he thought was true, then Oswald Piper's death was the most shockingly pointless one he had ever encountered.

Who does DI Radford suspect robbed the safe, and who does he suspect killed Oswald Piper?

Hints:

- Mark Swan has debts.
- Oswald Piper often boasted about his safe.
- Gwendolyn is only valuable to Mrs Piper.
- Catcher is squeamish.
- Only Katharine was sure Oswald had money in the saf.
- The murder and the robbery did not have to occur at the same time.

51. The Golden Empress

66 London isn't ready for jazz." Thought Mary Fitzgerald as she stood at the railing of the Empress of Britain as it left Southampton. "At least, most of it isn't. Yet."

Mary had always had a beautiful singing voice and her parents had paid for lessons and tutors aplenty. Maybe they thought she'd be the new Gracie Fields. She had thought that too, but then one day she had heard Fred Elizalde and his band on the BBC and her mind was blown. Jazz was wild, unpredictable yet so strangely familiar. She begged her parents to let her go to Paris, to New Orleans, to anywhere it was happening, and when they refused, she had found a group of other like-minded enthusiasts and tried to make a go of it. But it had been so difficult. People found jazz confusing or, if they read the papers, frightening. Appreciation for swing was growing but Mary had had so many doors slammed in her face. She knew it was a lot tougher for people who didn't have her background, her rich parents. But she was close to giving the whole thing up.

Which is why she was so excited about this trip. The RMS *Empress* was the largest ocean liner in the world, crossing the Atlantic in a week to Quebec, Canada with only first-class passengers onboard. And Mary was not a passenger, but instead a member of the crew! Except not exactly.

A booking agent had decided that among the other musical accompaniments of the journey a jazz band would be a good idea and so at the last minute Mary had found herself the chief female vocalist for "Jack Tavernier and his Tavern Boys". She wasn't familiar with the other members of the band, but they knew their stuff. They boasted that they'd played all the world's capitals, from Paris to Prague. Even more excitingly, apparently the BBC would be broadcasting their final performance, live from the Buccaneer's Ball on the last night of the voyage!

However, excitement had dissipated after the first night. The gig had gone well but she felt a distant from the band. Whether it was because she was a woman, or not a "real" jazz musician, she didn't know. They weren't unfriendly, just clearly already a tight unit, and not interested in making friends. The audience had also been small and lukewarm. She also thought she had spotted one of her father's friends, Sir Rodney Pettersen. Her dad was always taking trips to Sir Rodney's estate in Kilkenny. In fact, it was his patronage of the Royal Academy of Music that had helped Mary in the early days of her career. She thought he was watching with a look of distaste, but it might have just been concentration.

Now Mary was moving listlessly around the ship, not knowing any of the passengers and at a bit of a loose end. She nearly got in an argument with a Dutch man named Van Bruegel for shouting at one of the deckchair attendants but decided it wasn't worth it.

And then suddenly, around midday, a little man in a trench coat took her elbow and moved her quickly behind one of the deckchairs.

"Miss Fitzgerald, I thought that was you!" he exclaimed. "I must ask that you be discreet about my identity."

She had no idea who he was, so she just nodded.

"While I'm onboard you must address me as Mr Ian Dobson, not Detective Inspector!"

Of course, the investigator of the "Jazz Advertising Murders"!

"Good to see you again, Mr Dobson," she said teasingly.

"Since you have the potential to blow my cover, I am forced to take you into my confidence," he said and began explaining the situation.

Dobson and a few other officers were pretending to be members of the BBC crew who were onboard to set up the powerful new radio antenna needed to broadcast the concert. But his real purpose was to protect a large shipment of gold bullion that was being transported in the cargo hold!

"Nobody was supposed to know about it, but a few days ago we received information that indicated a criminal gang is on board, with a plan to steal it all!"

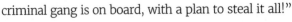

"Do you have any idea who?"

"Well, all the crew have had extensive background checks, so it has to be a passenger. But there's about 700 of them! I don't have the manpower to watch them all."

"Do you know anything else about the gang?"

Dobson shrugged. "Very little, our information came from a nose who had just overheard that they would be onboard, and they would be using some kind of signalling system. So, we've got people monitoring the radio room in shifts. But apart from that it's a bit like listening to jazz. I don't have a clue what's going on and I hate it."

Over the next day or so Mary and Dobson moved around the ship gathering information with the help of his officers, and by the evening they had what they felt were three likely suspects.

One was her father's friend, Sir Rodney! She didn't realize but Dobson said he had known associates in the Scottish underworld. And that castle definitely had a high upkeep cost, not helped by Sir Rodney's voracious gambling habit, as told to her by her father. He had also been seen lingering near the cargo hold many times with no real explanation, when he wasn't with his large group of companions.

The second was the Dutch man, Martin Van Bruegel. He apparently owned a string of pubs and night clubs in London and, as Dobson said, "you don't do that without rubbing elbows with some wrong'uns." Van Bruegel hadn't been near the cargo hold but he had a couple of supposed bodyguards who radiated menace, and Dobson said his contacts had claimed Van Bruegel's businesses had been struggling.

The third suspect, awkwardly, was Jack Tavernier, Mary's band leader. He wasn't always a musician, according to Dobson, and had been in and out of prison frequently. Mary hadn't noticed the band being particularly interested in the cargo hold but they had been keeping a distance with her.

Over the next couple of days Mary would perform with the band in the evening and try to gather more evidence with Dobson during the day. But it was very difficult to learn anything on a boat so packed with other people, especially as two of the suspects knew Mary personally and the Dutch man was suspicious of her. Dobson's limited officers already had their hands full monitoring the radio waves and guarding the cargo hold, so by the final day of the cruise they were none the wiser.

"They must be waiting until the Buccaneer's ball," Dobson said, pretending to twiddle some dials on the antenna's control board. "It makes sense, everyone's going to be dancing and extremely merry, plus the pirate costumes will serve as a good disguise."

"I can't help but feel the police could have thrown a few more resources at this, Mr Dobson," Mary said. "I'll be performing onstage; I won't exactly be able to keep an eye out."

"Come on, it's that jazz singing you're doing, isn't it?" said Dobson. "You could leave the stage in the middle of a song, and no-one would know the difference."

"Actually we'll be performing requests from the passengers," said Mary. "So I think people will be somewhat miffed if I stroll off before I finish their request."

On the night of the ball the ship was buzzing with excited passengers all wearing their most elaborate pirate costumes. They were shouting and waving cutlasses and threatening to keelhaul each other. A group of excitable bankers said they had spotted a smaller vessel following the ship at a distance in the mist and said they were going to "claim it for the Jolly Roger" but they were soon distracted by the buffet.

Dobson and his men had remained in their "BBC" civvies along with the actual BBC technicians, setting up microphones around the stage and making sure the antenna worked up in the radio room. Mary was wearing a subtle dress but had been asked to wear an eyepatch by the band.

"I hope that me having depth perception isn't part of your plan, Mr Dobson," said Mary.

"Just keep an eye out for anything funny," said Dobson. "I'll be trying not to let the jazz scramble my brain. I've taken the two men off guard duty so they can keep an eye on our suspects, so I hope this gamble pays off..."

Mary didn't think that was wise but didn't have time to say this as when they came onstage at 11pm Tavernier told her their first request had come in from Van Bruegel's group, apparently: Makin' Whoopee in the key of G.

As she sang and the band played, she peered into the crowd to see Van Bruegel's group but they didn't seem interested in the song at all, rather they were playing around with a series of pirates' scarves they had in red, white, and blue.

Tavernier told Mary next they'd be doing It Had To Be You.

"It's E major, boys, remember!" he told his band. "And put some mustard on it, Sir Rodney Pettersen's the one who asked for it!"

The Tavern Boys launched into the song with gusto and Mary felt even more pressure than before as she looked towards Sir Rodney's group, who were looking much more restrained in their pirate garb than others, essentially just wearing tricorn hats and tuxedos. Sir Rodney raised a glass to Mary, and she couldn't tell if his expression was merely friendly, or strangely gloating. Did he know what was going on? Dobson's surveillance had not exactly been subtle.

And so it went on through the night. Van Bruegel's group asked to hear Dinah in C Sharp, and then Sir Rodney's entourage pulled out the rather more obscure Nobody Knows You When You're Down And Out, a classic in A minor. At one point a group of merrymakers ran to the port side of the boat insisting they could see this mysterious ship in the darkness, but otherwise people were primarily drinking, dancing and drinking some more.

"Um, Miss, can I talk to you about your voice levels?" said Dobson in a ridiculous fake voice. In the corner he voiced his frustration.

"We've seen no sign of anything, Miss Fitzgerald. We think they're waiting for a particular time but no idea what that might be. And there's no sign of any signals going out over the radio."

"Have you noticed people have mentioned another ship out there, near this one?" asked Mary.

"Too much rum and excitement, I think," said Dobson. "Even if

they had a boat out there, they couldn't tell them anything, we're monitoring the airwaves like a hawk. Anything else seem odd?"

"I wonder if there's something going on with these song requests..." Mary said.

"Ooh, do you know The Liberty Bell March? No, I suppose that's not really a jazz song."

Tavernier gave Mary a whistle and she left Dobson to it and returned to the stage to sing I Ain't Got Nobody in B Flat, a request from Van Bruegel's group apparently.

"Hope we get to play Empty Bed Blues tonight," said Rick, a trumpeter, out of the corner of his mouth to Mary.

"Your choice?" she asked.

"Nah, it's Tavernier's, so he does solo accompaniment, and we can go get a drink!" said Rick.

"That'll be our set-capper, Rick," said Tavernier. "Last song. In F. So keep your lips on the trumpet and off the wine bottle."

The next request was Toot Toot Tootsie and when Tavernier told her it was from Sir Rodney again and she had to play it in C Sharp something clicked in her head. The key was in these songs, somehow. Looking around, she saw that both Van Bruegel and Sir Rodney couldn't be seen. Grabbing a napkin and her eyebrow pencil, she quickly wrote the songs down. Then she waved to Dobson and practically leapt off the stage.

"Initially I had no idea, but I've got it now. I know who's going to steal the gold, how they're signalling, and when they're going to do it!"

Who does Mary suspect is the leader of the criminal gang, what is their signalling method and when is it going to happen?

Hints:
- The robbers had to have someone to communicate with.
- Codes could be used to avoid detection.
- The time of the robbery is important.
- There is a type of communication which is not being monitored as closely.
- Together the songs have the key.
- But it may not be the keys of the songs.

SOLUTIONS

1. The Telltale Hands

Peter Dabbs killed Cedric Birtles. If, as Dabbs says, he was at work all day and he follows his time sheet obsessively, he would have noticed that the clock was running late, as it would have impacted his day. Therefore, he could not have been in the office. In fact, Birtles had fired Dabbs for laziness, including failing to wind the clock. Dabbs had been stewing in his hate all day before he went to the flat, killed Birtles, then broke in and stole the money to make it seem like a robbery.

2. Instinctive Detective

Ludwig is a female dog as evidenced by her having puppies, despite her name, yet the false Victor calls Ludwig he, and furthermore the dog seems to show only aggression to him. It is in fact Krendler, this time with much better makeup and a glued wig and moustache. He fought with Balanov over money and struck him in the head, then had to quickly impersonate him in the hope of getting Balanov's friends and family to lend him money due to his 'sickness'. The real Balanov was tied up at Krendler's house.

3. Indentation

Sumpter is innocent because Talbot and Winchester framed him. The bite mark on the statue is only on the top of the arm and Axton noticed there was nothing on the bottom, yet if you bite something you use both rows of teeth. He then noticed that the bronzed cast of Sumpter's teeth that Winchester was using as a paperweight had white powder on it and realised that they had used the cast on the statue to make it seem as if Sumpter had bitten it, hoping that by framing him for this crime they could prevent him from continuing to stalk them.

4. The Three Georges Paxman

Joe knows that the young man claiming to be George Paxman is the real one. Joe noted that the corpse had blue fluff on it that matched the navy argyle sweater Paxman was wearing and correctly surmised it formerly belonged to Alan.

He also noted that the discoloration on the amnesiac's mouth and chin indicates that he once had a beard that prevented that area from tanning, and that the body had a full beard and Paxman seems to be growing one. Furthermore, Paxman knows that the man in the bed was hit on the head and is a tramp, and while these things could be surmised from his situation and appearance, they all point to the truth: Paxman sought to fake his own death, so he knocked a homeless drunk on the back of the head, and dressed him in his clothes and items, roughly shaving him and hoping that the waterlogged corpse would be mistaken for him. Then he lured his friend Alan to his beach hut and killed him, stealing his clothes in the hope of impersonating him while on the run.

Under questioning Paxman confessed, revealing he'd learned the company was going to be investigated and he'd be in trouble. He thought Alan would stay undetected for weeks but when he saw the body being removed and realised the tramp had somehow survived, he felt his only option was to return to his real identity and claim the tramp was the criminal.

5. Deeper Freeze

Helen Parnacki thinks Enid Almond accidentally killed herself. The broken broom in the freezer was found by the door and Betty said the brooms had woodworm. Also, Enid had a young lover and Mr Almond has a big life insurance policy. She asked him to meet her at the factory propping the door open with a broom, hoping to lure him inside and close the door on him, leaving him to freeze to death. However, the broom handle snapped, and the door closed on her, and with no keys she couldn't get out.

6. Debutante in the Dark

Mary knows Giles Fontaine stole the necklace. He has an incredible sense of smell, and so was able to find where Felicity was because she was wearing the special perfume that he had created for her. His broad shoulders were the puffy shoulders of the pirate costume. Once arrested he confessed that he was greatly in debt and made a habit of stealing from his clients to fund his gambling.

7. Forbidden Fruit

Helen suspects that Malcolm poisoned Dennis with cyanide distilled from the cherry stones that they extract in the farm. He has chemistry knowledge and was the one who spearheaded the stone extraction. The village is contained, and no-one goes in or out, so he was forced to obtain the poison that way. Furthermore, even if there were trace amounts of cyanide in the stoned cherries Dennis had an all-meat diet and therefore did not eat cherries anyway. Under questioning Malcolm admitted that he hated the old man for forcing him to return to the farm and he thinks his family suspected the truth but turned a blind eye because they all hated the tyrannical old man as well.

8. No Ball

Radford thinks Tom Butcher created the exploding ball. As the ball has a short fuse it would need to be substituted for that bowl only. Butcher bowled directly at Braxton-Spummer instead of doing a bouncer like he normally would, and when asked why he claimed the weight was off, but Axton pointed out the weight would have been exactly the same. The chemical smell in the pigeon droppings suggest that it was drugged, and it provided a distraction from Butcher, who was always whistling (to indicate when the pigeon should be put on the pitch) and putting his hands in his pockets (to swap the match ball for his explosive replica.) When questioned Butcher confessed, saying he had been driven mad by his inability to bowl Braxton-Spummer out and had decided on a deadly solution.

9. Manual for Murder

Mary thinks Tony Grantham died in a crash but in Petunia's car! Tony's body had no signs of a steering column impact and there were also no signs of the braking. Furthermore, it's not common to drive around with a lot of fuel cans. While someone wearing Tony's outfit and goggles was seen limping into the garage the goggles could act as a disguise, and Petunia is almost the same height so could be her. Petunia's says her car is being repaired but they had planned to drive around drinking cocktails, so Mary thinks that Petunia drunkenly crashed her own car with Tony as the passenger. Then took his car, and swapped him into it and staged a different accident, using fuel cans to create a massive fireball. Under questioning she confessed, admitting she didn't know Celia had tinkered with the accelerator that had just been a stroke of luck.

10. Into A Corner

Joe thinks only Martin Belgeddes could have stolen the money, presumably to make a false insurance claim to cover the cost of the refurbishment. While there are boot prints in the paint on the way into the shop, there were no footprints in the paint on the way out of the shop. Considering that the paint was impossible to circumvent in any way, and there is only one entrance in and out of the building, then whoever knocked over the paint must have remained inside, and therefore only Belgeddes could be responsible.

11. Calling All Cars

Axton thinks that Captain McDonald is making the calls as a test of the system but forgot to tell anyone. Sergeant Longton says that McDonald is very enthusiastic about the system and is shut in his office. The man making the calls has an adult voice and he has a Scottish accent and Captain McDonald is Scottish. Each crime is different, suggesting that the calls are in the nature of trying to cover as many possibilities as possible, and as Barstow pointed out there was no benefit to him aggravating the police, which also implies that whoever is doing it is unaware of what's happening because otherwise they would have stopped so as not to antagonise the police further. It found that he was using a special set in his office to make the announcements, reading from test calls provided to him by the system's originator. Everyone agreed to pretend it had never happened.

12. Strange Developments

Mary thinks that Robert Murphy was not stabbing a person, but rather cutting an animal carcass. He owns a butcher shop that is small by his admittance, and Mrs Hall says about him going up to flat 4 and carrying heavy things back and forth and dropping metal hooks. The flat is cold and bare with blood on the floor suggesting that Murphy was storing animal carcasses in there because he did not have room at his shop. The holes in the ceiling were from the metal hooks used to hang them up, and Murphy's 'confession' wasmuch more in concern at being shut down for health violations than the words of a murderer.

13. The Unbandaged Man

Joe thinks the man is Omari Mostafa.

While it's true that there was no witness to Keats opening the sarcophagus and he has gambling debts that does not mean he has a motive to kill anyone.

Lois Nutt may have been suspected of poisoning her husband but the man in the sarcophagus evidently died of suffocation and hypothermia and she has no apparent motive either.

Furthermore, there are no signs of there having been a mummy at all. Joe also noted the scratch-marks, indicating the man was alive inside and died trying to get out, as well as a hole in the back drilled by modern hands that had become blocked up by packing material.

This all seems to indicate that the man must have entered the sarcophagus before it was transported using it to enter the country secretly. Drilling the hole to enable himself to breathe, and instructing the curator not to open it without the British museum assistance, as this would enable him to leave and escape when no-one was around. However, he had not anticipated that the airhole would become blocked and that the temperature in the plane's hold would be so low as to cause hypothermia, and he panicked and tried to get out but was unable, arriving at the museum already dead. The sand inside had blown in there from the desert storm. A call to the Egyptian authorities confirmed that Mostafa was a black-market antiques smuggler and was looking to escape justice.

14. The Missing Claret Jug

Axton is certain Frank Dittman stole the trophy.

All three of the suspects would have had opportunity to take it and both Smith and Dittman would be likely to know the safe combination due to Smith's time at the club and Dittman's 'friendship' with Leigh.

Leigh would derive no benefit from stealing it himself as he was hoping it would improve his standing and he would be personally held responsible for its loss.

Smith needed money but the Claret Jug is very famous and would be very difficult to sell. In addition, Smith refused to enter the clubhouse, had a minor coughing fit that was alleviated by using a device with a rubber bulb, all of which suggests he suffers from asthma, although he's trying to hide it. For this reason, he would be unable to go inside the dusty, sandy building site that the club has become.

However, while Dittman would not need to steal the trophy for money he resents Leigh, after repeatedly losing to him. If the trophy went missing it would impact Leigh badly. While Dittman claimed his shoes were sandy because he went in the bunker Leigh never saw that. Axton also noticed that Dittman's sand wedge had no sand on it, which is why he was testing to see how easily sand could be dislodged. Dittman's golf bag also looks very big and heavy, despite only being half full of clubs.

Under questioning Dittman admitted taking the trophy as a "prank", having laced the brandy with syrup of ipecac to give him a chance to go in and take it.

15. Who framed Bodger Mabbut?

Helen Parnacki suspects Cynthia Croom is lying and her husband did bequeath the painting to Bodger.

While Mabbut doesn't disagree when Mrs Croom says he's lying, it's clear he's not comfortable challenging his employer in public. Also, if he did intend on stealing the painting displaying it on the wall doesn't make any sense, neither does claiming it was bequeathed to him.

Ronson was previously a burglar and he's leaving soon so might need money, but beyond that he has no real motive for stealing it or framing Mabbut either, and as an experienced burglar he would surely know it's nearly impossible to fence a famous painting without getting caught.

However, Helen noticed that the shape in the wallpaper that marked where the cornfield was supposed to be was medium sized, while the painting itself is large, and although it's a painting of a landscape *The Cornfield* is portrait in orientation and the shape on the wall is landscape. She also noticed that the Dutch village painting that the constable found was medium-sized and had been propped up in the pantry.

While the lawyer said it hadn't been bequeathed Ronson implied that Mrs Croom used blackmail to get people to do what she wanted. Therefore, Helen thinks that Mrs Croom simply removed the Dutch village painting, hid it, then claimed *The Cornfield* had been there while all the time it had been on Mabbut's wall. This was confirmed by the lawyer who attested that Cynthia Croom had always been bitterly jealous of her husband's friendship with Mabbut.

16. Pack of Thieves

Mary thinks that the dealer, Alice Capewell, is cheating, with the approval of Sir James himself.

Geraldo Malfistoni would have little reason to cheat if he is rich, and while Sophie DeLange is more intelligent than she lets on she is correct that lipstick would be too visible on any cards to mark them. The judge does have a long fingernail, but he was losing and said that he enjoys the thrill of playing cards.

Considering all of the above could be lies Mary relied on what she knew. First, she knew that cards had gone missing and that was likely to be an employee. Then she noted that the judge said the issues with the game aided no one player, suggesting they aided the dealer and the club itself.

She had heard Sir John had financial problems, and thought it strange he would hire her to sing in his club, unless he wanted his customers distracted from Alice's activities. Furthermore, Nigel the nose scratcher was hired by Sir John, but his position would assist in sending messages to Alice more than being able to see any cheating. She also noticed Alice wiped dust off Sir John's cravat, a very familiar gesture between employer and employee, and when the judge had finished Sir John subconsciously positioned himself between Alice and the judge as if to protect her. She decided rather than reveal it publicly she would tell the men in private and shortly after Sir John gave up his ownership of the club.

17. Shattered Faith

Joe Hollobone believes the windows were broken by an escaped monkey.

Mrs Barchester certainly had the motive and anger to break the windows, but her attempt to throw her knitting at Joe showed that her arms were weak.

The boys in the cemetery seemed more preoccupied in searching for something, and the peanuts that Charlie had wouldn't be tough enough to break a window.

And the sailor that had been seen hanging around was also preoccupied in searching for something small, with a sack of fruit and a target with a red centre.

Joe remembered that all the panes of the stained glass that had been broken were red: the blood in the grail, the roses, the dragon and the cross in the English flag. He also remembered that Mrs Barchester had said she'd seen a 'hairy faced demon' in the cemetery. Knowing that sailors often had pet monkeys he surmised that the Greek sailor had one that had run away, one he had trained to throw stones at the red target. Monkeys love fruit and peanuts in the shell are often known as monkey nuts. Joe found the sailor again and with the help of the local boys managed to convince the monkey to return to him.

18. A Sign of Character

Helen thinks that it was the poorly maintained factory that led to Tom getting injured.

Leaving Tom's reported comment aside there's no motive for either Adam or Billy to hit him, and Norman Pitkin saw them both together, providing them with an alibi.

When Pitkin handed her the 'magnet' that didn't work she realised what had happened. Magnets traditionally have a U shape, and it was a U-shaped piece of metal Norman had found, and she remembered that the sign read 'H BERT CONFECTIONARIES', missing the letter U. She then realised that what Tom was saying wasn't 'It was you!' but 'It was U!', and this also explained his talk about letters while in hospital. The U had fallen off, hitting him on the head, then bouncing into the canal like so many other parts of the crumbling factory, to be found by Norman. She immediately arranged for increased security around the factory and compensation for the boy's family.

19. The Supper Club

Helen Parnacki thinks that Giuseppe Beretti stole the pate.

Both Rustin and Digby had the opportunity to steal it, except that it was Beretti who sent them off elsewhere, rather than their own suggestion.

Beretti was already opposed to the idea of opening the tin, but the thing that clinched it for Parnacki was the knowledge that canned food wasn't invented until the early 19th century, and that the dodo went extinct in 1681, over 100 years before then! When Beretti received this news, he rushed out of the room, seemingly in a fury but actually to conceal his realisation that the tin must be a fake! Having sent Rustin and Digby off he opened the tin to find only rotten sardines and tipped them into the bin, relying on the two young men's mutual suspicion to lead them to think each other was the thief. After Parnacki explained this Beretti came clean, saying he felt a fool for being conned this way, and surprisingly she found the two young men forgave him, deciding that they were going to change the supper club to a mystery solving club!

20. Garden of Horrors

Joe Hollobone thinks Felicity is alive and well and not inside the plant.

Dr Netherton certainly has motive and a thorough dislike of Felicity Barbas, and his wife's alibi might be ruled to be biased, but if he believed the plant to be valuable, he'd be unlikely to either risk its health by pushing her into it, or even by claiming she was inside, as he'd surely know that eventually someone would decide to cut it open.

Felicity's boyfriend might be unhappy about his paper's fortunes, but it doesn't make sense that he would kill her as his frequent visits suggest they are still very much in love.

However, Joe noticed a few strange things about this plant. Firstly, even though it's supposedly from a tropical climate, the room is colder than the other rooms or the Palm House, but tropical plants need warm humid environments. Its main pod is a different colour to its leaves, not unusual but indicative of something. Furthermore, the notes advising people not to touch it conveniently mean that it's very difficult to inspect the plant closely.

Joe also felt it was odd that when the truck arrived Felicity was immediately there with the scissor lift trolley when it had been established that the plant was unexpected, and they had not even phoned ahead. The truck was also described as unusually small.

Remembering the old newspapers at the house led Joe to the conclusion that the plant itself was a fake made from papier mache, which he proved by cutting it open. It's possible the plant and leaves underneath were real (hence the difference in leaf colours) but the unusually large plant was created to be an exciting front-page story for the newspaper where her boyfriend worked, and the idea she had been swallowed was added for extra impact. The human sized inside was also papier mache and some old clothes. Felicity and her boyfriend were found soon after at a local pub, laughing at the success of their hoax.

21. Hard To Convey

Helen Parnacki thinks Agnes Sudwell did it, to save Mr McNamara's life.

Sally Green and Marjory Cook had witnesses proving they didn't do it. William Kenneths has the motive, but as he pointed out he was too far back to be able to throw a pie tin in there, being a supervisor and not working on the belt.

Gregory MacNamara may have been annoyed at Wright & Downing over the money dispute but there was no benefit to him breaking the belt if it injured his workers and stopped production and furthermore, he seemed to actually like the belt.

Miss Parnacki noted that pie tins (like the one thrown into the machine) were applied at the end of the belt, which is where Agnes Sudwell and Mr MacNamara were. She found a pair of scissors and a pentagonal piece of striped silk. She remembered that Agnes was often seen carrying sharp objects and that Mr MacNamara was no longer wearing a tie, and admonished Downing for the fact that workers had to 'lean over' the conveyor belt, and she also remembered that workers usually wore overalls.

From these clues she calculated that Mr MacNamara had been leaning over and his tie had got caught in the belt, causing him to make the 'sudden strangled cry of pain' that Kenneths heard. Thinking quickly, Agnes threw the pie tin into the works to stop the machine and used the scissors to snip his tie free, the pentagonal piece of striped silk being the end of the tie.

When questioned MacNamara admitted that this is what had happened and felt embarrassed about it, which is why he covered it up and gave Mrs Sudwell the day off out of gratitude. Mr Downing agreed not to reveal this and went off to develop a tie-proof conveyor belt.

22. The Great Train Robbery

Constable Axton thinks that the Scotsman is still in the station's sidings, and Robert Stephenson put it there.

The hole in the fence having been cut from the inside indicates that it must have been either Pink, Dankworth or Stephenson. They all had the opportunity and motive to take the Scotsman. Pink seems to adore it and wants to drive it. But he is also a working director and would get opportunities to do that during the filming.

Dankworth has a criminal brother, but he indicated he had no connection with them anymore, and his comment about being 'good with figures' made Axton wonder if Dankworth was responsible for his brother's tax details being shared with the authorities.

The Scotsman had not been seen leaving the station at any point, and it also requires a full crew to operate for any length of time. It's possible one of the three could have allowed confederates into the station and they stole it but driving the world's most recognisable train around seems like a foolish endeavour.

Axton then reasoned it must have been disguised. The fake shack was being painted with black paint and many cans had gone missing. While the Flying Scotsman has a distinctive 'Darlington Green' coloured engine the standard locomotives are coloured black.

At that point Axton realised that if the engine had been painted black there was no reason to take it out of the station at all, it could simply be hidden amongst the decommissioned old locomotives on the siding.

The only one of the group who could alter the manifest would be Stephenson, who could then scrap the locomotive, get the money and inconvenience his rivals at the same time. Stephenson was also very tired, as anyone who stayed up all night painting a train black might be, and furthermore had red scrubbed hands he was at pains to conceal. Once questioned he confessed and also added that he hated trains because of being teased about his famous origins at school and relished the chance to scrap such an iconic engine.

23. Vicious Cycle

Mary thinks Brian Roth is the Soho Slasher, but not deliberately.

"Knives" Niven might be a criminal with a blade-based nickname, but he has no blades on his wheels and in his line of business random violence would draw attention, and his nickname is based on his last name.

Philomena Winsop has a lot of manic motivation but does not seem to have any violent tendencies and she too has no blades on her wheel.

The only person whose wheels they did not see was Brian Roth, and when Philomena mentioned "the broken wheel of piety" it made Mary think about the accident Roth had earlier in the day when he crashed into the sign and she suddenly wondered if maybe the "slasher" wasn't doing it deliberately but by accident with a broken wheel, drunkenly riding around and then losing his bike. Mary and Constable Rossini returned to his house and helped him find the bike which did indeed have several broken spokes. Once sober he made reparations towards the people he'd hurt.

24. Quid's In

Helen Parnacki suspects Owen Dearmans is the embezzler.

While the whole affair was started by Phripps (and Miss Parson's) elaborate spending, it would be stupid to flash money around if you were embezzling as Twill acknowledged. Phripps refused to say anything more than 'petunias', but Miss Parnacki remembered that Miss Parsons said he would usually have dirt under his nails and talk a lot about his aunt until a certain day, and that he also then had much more money, and wore black for a while, which suggests a bereavement and possibly an inheritance. Parnacki spoke to Phripps, and he confirmed his aunt had left him a large sum in his will because of his kindness, including helping with the petunias in her garden, and he didn't want to talk about it because he was genuinely upset.

Owen Dearmans wanted to be an investor, but his father wouldn't permit it. He returned from Australia after 3 years of working for a 'mineral excavation and extraction company', or a mining company, in other words, and therefore the word MINE on the records could refer to an investment that Dearmans made with the firm's money, paying it back after he'd taken his profits but accidentally giving back one pound more than he 'borrowed'. Owen confessed this and his father, torn between firing him and being proud of his acumen and guts, decided to promote him to 'Head of Australian Sales'.

25. Rare Old Mountain Dew

Constable Axton suspects Arthur Veil of killing Peter Mallon.

Walsh and Veil accuse each other of owning the still and Cleaver doesn't confirm either story. As Peter was apparently left alone at the end of the night, he would be vulnerable for attack from any of the men. However, Cleaver says his wife would confirm that he came home.

It seems as if Arthur Veil couldn't have attacked Peter because he went blind and had to be led home.

However, Veil says that "later the weathervane showed the wind was blowing North-East" leading him to worry about a possible fight. If Veil had been blinded by the potcheen he wouldn't be able to see that. Therefore, he was lying about it and could have snuck back when the others had gone and attacked Peter. He eventually confessed, saying Peter had been blackmailing him with the threat of exposure for months.

26. Cold Blood

Joe Hollobone suspects Jane Heep killed her husband.

Kurt Weiss has a clear dislike for Tobin Heep, but he has an alibi from 9am. And Mrs Heep says she was out of the building since 9:30am.

Kevin Link has a criminal past and says he delivered the ice block at 10:30am, but Mrs Heep says it was meant to be delivered at 4:30pm, and the block in question does not seem melted enough to have been delivered at 10:30am. He also says that Tobin Heep chipped off some ice for a cocktail, when Heep doesn't drink. This all seems very incriminating.

However, as Link points out, robbing a customer of the job he works at would be very stupid especially if you're an experienced criminal. If Link was telling the truth, why would Heep chip off ice for a cocktail? Possibly for his wife, who hadn't actually left yet. She claimed he was kind but both Link and Weiss say he was mean. So, after Link has left at 10:30 she stabs Tobin Heep and then using his key hides the ice in Tobin's flat which is so dark and cold it will keep it from melting as much. She goes out shopping, then on her return puts the ice back to make it seem like Link was lying and frame him for the crime. A police search eventually found the gold watch at a pawn shop where she had left it to fund her spending spree.

27. The Stings

Mary Fitzgerald thinks the two men are in fact police officers.

The dame's arrival from elsewhere proves she wasn't being kept captive in the house. It's possible she was being held captive elsewhere but that doesn't explain why the two men were remaining in her garden with the (possibly) fake wasps' nest.

The men had clean, shiny shoes, good posture, and greeted Mary with 'Can I help you.' They were both moustached and one of them paced the garden like he was on the beat. They were frequently going up the ladder, and they seemed alarmed at the idea of the girls talking to Lord Marchant-Whyte, the importer from Bolivia, and it was after this conversation that they seemed to 'summon' the Dame to calm the girls down.

Therefore, Mary felt it made sense that they were policemen there to conduct surveillance on Lord Marchant-Whyte (looking into his garden using the ladder) with the wasp's nest as the excuse for their presence. Philomena said that the Dame was often vigilant and talking to the police so it made sense she might give them permission to use her house this way.

Mary recommended Philomena stay out of it for now, and soon enough Lord Marchant-Whyte was arrested and they read in the papers how the local police had managed to expose an enormous cocaine smuggling ring in the area.

28. Ragpicker's End

Constable Axton suspects that Aksel Holmboe killed Henry Wellbelove.

Jemima Green called the blackmailer an 'old miser', which implies knowledge of his identity, but she knew a woman who was blackmailed by him 40 years earlier so it makes sense that she would assume he was old.

Paul Polder was a former violent criminal, but Wellbelove's death was not violent, and Polder also seems to be under the impression that the blackmailer was a member of the criminal fraternity like he formerly was, whereas Wellbelove operated on his own with no connections.

Aksel Holmboe claimed he did not pay Wellbelove, but his secret was not exposed so this was clearly untrue. Furthermore, Radford and

Axton saw him burning all of his rubbish as part of his daily routine, an unusual act unless you had already realized it was being used to spy on you and decided to burn it all to prevent that ever happening again. Under questioning Holmboe admitted that he had seen Wellbelove combing through rubbish when he was awake at 4am and had followed him back to the yard and killed him with the poison he used to keep mice out of the bakery.

29. The Second Mouse Gets the Cheese

Mary thinks the unconscious man is the narcoleptic Dadaist artist.

None of the possible suggested ideas make any real sense. You would not set up mousetraps to trap a man, and the 'fountain' is already gone, and why is the man unconscious anyway?

The Duc hates the artwork but has no reason to set up hundreds of mousetraps.

Reeves has been stealing wine but why would he trap a man there after taking the fountain? Calvin Petty II needs money but again why mousetraps? It's illogical.

That's when Mary realised the answer lies not with logic but with art. Calvin Petty is constantly commissioning new artworks and one of the people, he works with is a narcoleptic Dadaist artist, like Marcel Duchamp. The mousetraps could be a new artwork, and the man at the centre the artist, fallen asleep spontaneously. At first it seems impossible he could have set the mousetraps up around himself, but then she realised he could have set them up from the outside to the inside, backwards. When Calvin Petty arrived, he confirmed this was the case and that the 'fountain' had been stored away in an annex of the castle.

30. London's Burning

Constable Axton suspects Millicent Marville of burning the model.

Duncan Hamm might have reasons to resent Meriwether, but he wants to have the model, not burn it, he has an alibi from his wife, and furthermore wouldn't have the expertise to burn the model without burning the shed.

Gareth Clegg was an arsonist and so has the skills and the

inclination, but even if he is lying about reforming, he also has an alibi.

Millicent's motivation for burning the model is clear as she feels it has a power over her father and without it, he might spend more time in the real world. She also has knowledge about arson from talking with Gareth Clegg. Furthermore, Axton noticed that she mentioned that the Clock Tower on the Houses of Parliament was synchronised with the real time, and yet Meriwether had only just installed that feature before he went to bed. If Millicent had only seen the model years before she would not have seen that detail. She admitted as much when she was questioned, and her father chose not to press charges.

31. The Seven Hags

Joe Hollobone suspects that Ezekiel Arnecourt took the seventh Hag because of his religious beliefs.

Paul might have a motive in that the story would bring publicity, but their tourist trap isn't set up yet, and he's correct that it would upset the locals and historians. He also doesn't have any means of moving the stone.

Aleister Crowley might be a noted 'wicked person' and self-declared magician but he's clearly a publicity seeking charlatan with no means of taking the stone.

Ezekiel claims not to be religious, but Crowley did notice that Ezekiel avoided blaspheming, and he named his Suffolk Punch horses Gog and Magog, a biblical reference. They would be big and strong enough to move the standing stone. Furthermore, the slurry pit is now overflowing, as if a large object had been thrown into it. Ezekiel himself said he thought it better that the standing stones would be disrupted. After Joe put this to him Ezekiel admitted he had 'broken the devil's circle' and said that his son was welcome to retrieve it from the slurry pit personally.

32. Who Watches the Watchmakers?

Detective Inspector Radford suspects Peter George stole the watch.

All of the guests have a motive, so it comes down to opportunity. Comments from Philip Twice and Darius Vaughn reminded Radford that gentlemen usually remove their jacket when playing billiards, meaning Messingham's jacket with the key inside was hung up there.

It's possible one of the men could have 'swapped' their jacket with Messingham's, but that would only have given them the key, and they would not have been able to take it from the dresser when his study was in full view of the billiard table. So, the only way to successfully take it would be at a time when one of the men was alone in that part of the house.

If Messingham was getting Brandy from 8:15– 8:20, Vaughn was in the lavatory from 8:08–8:19, and Philip Twice was on the phone from 8:16–8:34, that means Peter George was alone in the billiard room from 8:16–8:19, and as he established, he is quick, that is just about enough time for him to get the key and steal the watch. Radford's theory was confirmed when he found the watch after searching George's pockets.

33. Fowl Play

Helen Parnacki suspects that Harriet Dootson killed Bob Dootson and the chickens, albeit possibly by accident.

Donnie Birtwell clearly disliked Bob Dootson and was preparing to act on it. But it's unlikely he would do anything to harm chickens.

Sandy Cronshaw seemed to think Dootson's death would relieve him from his duties on the farm, but he has an alibi for the time of the death.

Harriet Dootson considers herself an inventor, particularly using electricity, and she suggested putting a metal floor into the hen house. She also seemed to be concerned about the hens wandering around and not being in their nests. Bob Dootson was also notable for being barefoot much of the time.

Therefore, Helen thinks it's possible that Harriet had rigged an electrical circuit to the henhouse floor to deter the hens from stepping on it. She either used too high a voltage and didn't anticipate Bob entering the house and getting shocked, or she planned it that way to get rid of him. The burns that might have been visible on his feet were concealed by the considerable callouses. Harriet eventually confessed saying that it was an accident, and she hoped her next prototype wouldn't be quite so strong.

34. Oh No You Didn't...

Mary Fitzgerald thinks it was Kay Bartholomew-Keen.

Robinson Coy is clearly prepared to commit crimes and is reportedly a good runner, but Mary suspects he was about to say "I lost money on the race" because the horse that won was a rank outsider, and so it wouldn't benefit him to help them cheat.

Tom Tildrum would obviously be a likely suspect due to his connection to his brother and his Olympic background, but he is unfit and also seems to have a spiky relationship with his brother that would make their working together in the costume unlikely.

Kay Bartholomew-Keen was quick to dismiss the race's outcome as "blatant cheating" but this was after it was clear that the victory would not be accepted. He does not have a verifiable alibi. Most importantly, although he claims his leg is broken, he is using his crutch on the side with the broken leg, when you must use the crutch on the other side, so as to balance your body weight correctly. It was soon discovered that his cast was in fact a fake and he had helped them win so that he could collect on a large bet on Timmerary Tip.

35. Bad Appetite

Constable Axton thinks Quentin Freemont is responsible for Gregory Harlow's death, but not deliberately.

Robin Martin might not be telling the truth about Gregory blackmailing him, and he could have put the poison in in the kitchen, but as Axton points out, killing him at his own restaurant would no doubt accelerate any exposure of his secret.

Polly will inherit her husband's money, but it she controlled it anyway.

As the poison was only present in the baklava, then it stands to reason that Gregory ate the baklava, not the parfait. Axton noted that Polly said that her husband was bad with words, and then quickly attempted to cover her comment. Gregory's notebook was blank, and Quentin noticed that Polly often had a notebook of her own. They would also often eat the same meals, but in this situation that would not be possible as only one parfait was made per day. This leads to the conclusion that it was in fact Polly who wrote Gregory's reviews! She would make her own notes from eating the same dish as him, but couldn't do that this time, so they had to swap. Quentin intended to kill Polly, his rival, and poisoned her food with arsenic he got from his pharmacy job, going to the bathroom as a cover, so he didn't see that they swapped plates. Gregory's dying words were not 'bad' but 'bak...', trying to say baklava. Quentin cracked under questioning, and the guilt that he had killed his beloved mentor.

36. One-Act Tragedy

Mary does think Laurence Chance killed Phyllida Montrose, but she thinks the Kensington Theatre society is truly responsible.

The dagger is the most vital detail. Laurence stabbed Phyllida in full view of everyone, that's undeniable, and despite his stunned state seems to acknowledge that, but his reaction might not be that of a love-crazed fiend but rather someone who didn't realise they were actually going to commit a murder.

Gideon Key admits they took laudanum, but Mary knows it doesn't tend to make you violent. The Kensington Theatre people claimed Laurence was madly in love with Phyllida, but Key instead said he never mentioned her and wasn't romantic, more obsessed with experiences. Laurence told Mary that he wanted to know what it was like to kill, and Gideon told her how if he couldn't experience things for real, he'd simulate them, like the avalanche. When she asked about the dagger's origins he had only angrily said 'A mean trick.'

Therefore, Mary came to the horrifying conclusion that Laurence had approached the theatre group and asked them if they would help him simulate a murder. For some reason, possible the 'secrets' of theirs that Georgia Winterbourne alluded to, they decided instead to turn a fake murder into a real one, and gave him a real dagger instead of the trick one they had promised, so when he stabbed her in the park he was stunned and horrified to learn what he had done, and they had trusted that if he told the truth his reputation as a 'drug fiend' would protect them.

With that in mind, Mary confronted Georgia Winterbourne and convinced her to confess, and incriminate the rest of the group.

37. The Hermit of Thrunton Wood

Helen Parnacki suspects that the Earl of Northumberland killed Old Harry.

Brynwel Jones had reason to resent the hermit due to his poaching but seems to care for him. Matthew Arkwright was drunk and went off to go to the toilet but claimed he didn't fire the gun.

Then Helen remembered that the Earl claimed to be able to tell Arkwright's gun had not been fired, even though he professes to know nothing about guns. He also said that Arkwright wasn't gone long enough to go to Old Harry's shack, but nobody is supposed to know where the shack is, especially a man who claims to have no interest in the hermit. Furthermore, while Arkwright and Jones' absences are reported to be fairly short the Earl's absence to 'pursue a bird' has no time limit on it.

Helen remembered that the cook had said how she previously worked for 'the three of them', being the Earl, his brother and their sister, but now it was just the Earl and his sister and their party guests. What happened to his brother? Jones said he thought Old Harry was intelligent. What if he was the missing brother? That would explain his last words, 'I'm the first...", claiming to be the first Earl?

Helen discreetly sent these thoughts to Canker's superior in a fair forgery of Canker's handwriting, and the investigation was forced to arrest the Earl. It became apparent that his brother had suffered greatly in the War and become a hermit with the Earl taking over, but he couldn't allow his brother's existence and presence to jeopardise his profitable shooting parties, so he took Jones' gun and shot him during his time away from the party.

38. Park Royal Rock

Joe Hollobone suspects Sid Prowse made the sticks of rock.

Arthur Moult, as the machine's creator, would have the know-how but doesn't have a motive as he is building another machine elsewhere.

Maria Alphonse does seem to be acting suspiciously. But Joe remembered Giuseppe's comment about a pocketful of sugar being enough to make candy floss, and Maria hanging around near the sugar supplies with trousers suggests to him she's syphoning off the supplies to his competitors, not printing strange sticks of rock.

Sid Prowse claimed he was only on night shift to avoid his wife, but he revealed she works in a night club, which is also a night job. She also has connections with Sammy MacTavish, a gangster who runs gambling, and Maria said how two "jocks" or Scottish men tried to collect the sticks, only to realize they were meant to collect them at "PM, not AM", meaning they were meant to collect them from Prowse. Prowse claims not to understand the machine, but Arthur Moult said everyone at the factory thinks it's a manufacturing device, but Prowse correctly called it an analyzer, suggesting he would know how to program it to print out random numbers. Prowse eventually confessed everything, and Joe used his connections to ensure Giuseppe would be left alone. These were to serve as "tickets" for an illegal lottery.

39. The Zoo Mystery

Helen suspects Phyllis James stole the jewellery, or rather, the mongoose she called Richard stole it for her.

Helen dismissed Gordon McLeish immediately, like his lions he was too proud and self-important. Also, he was very cautious when going into cages with the animals, always having a back-up keeper with him, who would have seen him handling any stolen goods.

David Breslaw was shifty and uncomfortable when being questioned and he was also small and wiry, so the right build for a burglar. However, he was timid and terrified of authority and his whole demeanour suggested he would never have the courage to commit one theft let alone a string of them.

This left Phyllis James. Not only did she have the means, but the motive as well. First of all because she had a rapport and access to all the animals' cages where the loot was concealed. Secondly, her special bond with Richard the mongoose would allow her to use him to gain entry to the large houses that were robbed. He could get in and out undetected and could be trained to bring her the 'shiny' objects she wanted. The other clue that pointed to the mongoose was the mangled snake brooch, as mongooses detest snakes. Thirdly her motivation was to get enough funds to have her own zoo.

Helen had a sneaking admiration for Phyllis James' skills and determination, but felt duty bound to pass her theory onto Inspector Frank. He dismissed it out of hand, as she always suspected he would.

40. The Sorrell Sisters

Joe Hollobone thinks Rebecca Sorrell must inherit Sorrell Hall.

Rachel claims her aunt meant to leave it to her, but she has no evidence. Rosalind claims she's the oldest, and if the will is declared invalid it makes sense she would inherit, but apart from not mentioning the other sisters there is no evidence that Arabella Sorrell was not of sound mind.

However, Joe Hollobone was very aware of the fact that Philip Kerslaw had not met any of these women, only received letters. Each of the women, despite their wildly differing personalities, began the letter by saying 'One...', and furthermore seemed to know what the others were writing even though they claimed to live totally separate. He had noted in fact that the house was designed so that living separate would not really be possible. This is what led him to the conclusion that all three sisters are in fact different personalities of the same woman. Rebecca is the real sister, and Rosalind and Rachel are alternate personality states. Rachel is as assertive and dominant as she would hope to be, and Rosalind as creative and free-spirited.

Kerslaw was able to refer Rebecca to a psychoanalytic clinic in Vienna.

41. The Jazz Advertising Murders

Norman Satner committed the Jazz Advertising Murders.

Dobson's only reason for suspecting Mary is her association with Jazz and her determination to find the truth, and if you've read any of her previous stories you will understand why she was taking steps to investigate the murder of her friend De Lonnel.

Duncan Philips did seem unconcerned about their deaths, but he was concerned about their negative impact on the campaign, so why would he commit them?

What Dobson seemed to miss, and Mary tried to tell him about, was that all the murders were staged to look like the posters from the campaign. Giles Markwell wearing black tie and tails on a black and white striped rug in Harrods echoes the tuxedoed man dancing on a piano, Lucinda Principal hanging from the neon sign of Sunset Frozen Foods with a hairbrush tied to her hand reflects the singer in front of the sunset, and the scene of Paul De Lonnel's murder was The Trumpet pub, with the crumpled-up song sheets reflecting the musical notes of the trumpeter. Whoever committed these murders has a very visual mind, which suggests Norman Satner, who was constantly doing drawings, whereas Duncan Philips readily admitted he has no sense of visuals at all. Furthermore, their deaths would benefit Satner as Philips admitted that they meant the successful mustard campaign would have to stop and Satner's campaign for Gentlemen's Relish (a rival condiment) would have more of a chance.

Dobson arrested Mary and it was only while interrogating her that he got the opportunity to hear her theories and could be convinced to get the right culprit.

42. Kind Hearts and Correlations

The Parnackis think that David Franchester killed Philip Franchester.

In the absence of a signature and any other way of telling who wrote the confession there has to be another indicator of its author. Ethel tld Helen to think about symbols and David said that the group used symbols as signatures. There's a triangle on the confession, so whose symbol was that?

Ethel's room is filled with circles: Doilies, plates and clocks, and she mentions her sewing circle.

Ronald Arbor is heavily associated with squares. He was often in the square boxing ring, wore a checked suit and travelled 'the four corners of the Earth.'

Friar David, however, seems connected with triangles, from the poster of the holy trinity and the pyramid to the three petals of a clover and the shape of a mountain. Therefore, he is most likely to have written the confession. Helen returned to him, and he admitted he poisoned Philip as

43. The Three Riddles

Mary suspects that George Swanson is behind the mysterious riddle business.

Out of the three riddles, George's is the only one that seems guessable. It's also the only one written in rhyme, like the note that

Cedric left Mary. The other two seem to be random collections of food. Mary noted that George liked food as he was piling it up at the buffet, and also he liked pranks as shown by the hand buzzer. She also remembered that Charlotte told her that the family lawyer had been distracted by a whoopee cushion when getting the riddles. Cecil didn't like rude pranks so it must have been someone else.

Mary thinks that as George knew their father was doing the riddles he prepared fake ones for his siblings, distracted them all with the cushion and swapped them out, as a final prank! Mary and the sisters confronted their brother and he happily confessed and gave them the real riddles, and by the end of the day they all had gold coins and a good laugh.

And the solution to George's riddle? His name!

44. We Write in Water

Helen has come to the conclusion that the college scout, Henry O'Hara murdered Basil Michaelmas.

The former student, Richard Malahide, had a strong motive as it was a combination of O'Hara and Michaelmas who had ganged up to have him sent down from Oxford. He was also in the room when everyone else arrived, so he also had the opportunity. However, naughty boy that he is, he was too shocked and wasn't even brave enough to answer Helen's questions, let alone do the professor in.

Torquil Hardy-Morris also had plenty of motive, he quite clearly despised Michaelmas, and was more than happy to see his demise. He was also extremely angry at the plagiarism and the shame it might bring on Brasenose colleges reputation. He did not have much opportunity though, as he had spent most of his time between the argument he had with Basil, and his return to the study where the dead man was found, with Helen Parnacki.

O'Hara said that Michaelmas had plagiarised his article and when confronted by Hardy-Morris, Michaelmas had immediately admitted it, even though he must have known it would destroy his career. But both O'Hara's version and Michaelmas' version were written on the same typewriter. Why would Michaelmas go through the trouble of typing it all out again, especially as O'Hara said his name wasn't even on it? He could simply have submitted it as his own.

This made Helen realise that maybe Michaelmas did write the article after all, and O'Hara somehow forced him to pretend he'd plagiarised it. She remembered that Michaelmas had had a brief scandal in his youth and that O'Hara's father knew him then, and perhaps something O'Hara's father had told him about it had enabled O'Hara to blackmail Michaelmas into the scheme. Then when Michaelmas confronted him, saying he'd changed his mind, O'Hara stabbed him with the pen, trying to frame Malahide.

Helen sent an anonymous typewritten letter to the police and O'Hara was arrested trying to flee the country hours later.

45. Nothing to Mend

Joe Hollobone suspects Madame Benoit is trying to kill Wilfred.

All three of the people there have possible motives: Both Madeleine and Trevor stand to get money from Wilfred and may wish to have him out of the way so they can be together, and Madame Benoit would also be able to enjoy Wilfred's money through her daughter.

So for Joe it comes down to who seems most likely to be a murderer? Madame Benoit's two previous husbands both died, one in definitely mysterious circumstances. And it was she who met Wilfred first, not Madeleine, introducing the two of them. She was seen compulsively touching a lot of rings on her left hand, which is traditionally where engagement rings are kept. This all points to the possibility that Madame Benoit is what they call a "black widow" killer, murdering husbands to acquire their money. She saw Wilfred as another possible target but considering the heat still being on from her previous husband decided that it would be better if Madeleine marry him instead and then she could bump him off when they were back in the UK.

Once Joe communicated this Wilfred announced that after he called the police on Madame he was going abroad under an assumed identity, and that Madeleine and Trevor were welcome to each other!

46. Stinging Nettles

Axton is convinced that Margaret Purefoy is blackmailing her little sister.

Brandon Forsythe has a strong motive as Wilhelmina Nettles was going to use a new agent for her new book series. He also lives in Brighton where the letters were posted, but he lacked opportunity.

James Purefoy was quite obviously in love with his sister-in-law and would do her bidding. He also spent time at the cottage doing odd jobs so might have discovered the drawings. However, whether he would resort to blackmail to try and win more of her affections is pretty debateable.

The strongest candidate is Margaret, her sister, who Wilhelmina treated as her personal chattel, as she did with most people who came into her orbit. So, she had a strong personal motive. Not only was she used by the more successful sister who she must have resented, the author even stole the name of her doll for her great creation! She also engineered the opportunity by taking Wilhelmina Nettles to the book signing. The two hours she was there gave Margaret ample opportunity to go back to the cottage and stage a robbery. She would have noticed where the drawings were kept as she cleaned the place. Her resentment of her sister had been exacerbated even more by the hold she had over Margaret's husband, James.

The unequivocal sentiment in her last note: "IF YOU WANT THEM BACK YOU WILL PAY, IF YOU DON'T, YOU WILL PAY!", smacked of someone more interested in revenge than money.

Radford and Axton followed up their hunches and arrested Margaret, who broke down and confessed, however Wilhelmina, in an act of compassion, refused to press charges and her sister was let off with a severe reprimand. Wilhemina also sent Constable Axton a signed original illustration of Tippy the Tortoise.

47. The Final Sonata

Mary thinks Apollo Bardsley did kill himself.

While Francesca benefited the most financially from his death and also gained freedom from his control she was at the doctors and had several witnesses and had not been part of his life for a while anyway.

Baker also benefited financially, and the will was changed to benefit him at the last minute, but he loved Apollo and immediately went to work for someone else despite his stipend, so is clearly not concerned about independence.

His brother Benjamin might have killed him so that he could escape being in his shadow, but he was climbing Kilimanjaro at the time, and he also pointed out that even in death Apollo eclipsed him.

In fact, Apollo killed himself because he was beginning to suffer from arthritis of the hands, particularly his left due to excessive use. His father suffered from the same and arthritis can be hereditary. He had many secret appointments and phone calls and had a cabinet Francesca could not enter that had medicine inside. He began using a typewriter to disguise his poor handwriting and repeatedly called off concerts for spurious reasons, refusing even to play in front of his wife should she figure it out. He was obsessed with strength and his legacy and refused to let anyone know he had the problem, preferring to take his own life and rely on Baker to keep it quiet with the stipend providing motivation. But he was unable to use his left hand to fire the gun and was forced to use his right.

48. Dumb Witness

DI Radford thinks Dora Affanberk killed Henry Gottle.

Cheeky Charlie had motivation to kill Gottle and had 20 minutes in which to kill him. He said he was smoking a cigarette, but he seemed to be lying and there were no witnesses. But Radford remembered that Charlie mostly seemed reluctant to talk in front of Sherrinford Cook and asked to speak privately, and also looked particularly guilty when Cook mentioned Charlie talking to his wife. Radford surmised that Cheeky Charlie had in fact been with Cook's wife during that time and that's why he lied.

Sherrinford Cook had multiple witnesses to his activities that evening so he couldn't have done it.

Brian Affanberk/The Great Afanti also had a motive to kill Henry Gottle, especially after Gottle mocked him using the dummy. He was a former knife thrower and it seemed that Henry Gottle had put up a poster to provoke him about that. He even predicted a death! And during the period between Gottle's voice being heard at 8:20, and his going on stage at 8:30, he claimed to be meditating. Radford doubts he is a genuinely spiritual person, so he feels this is not a solid alibi. But Miss Dill heard a vacuuming noise coming from the dressing room and it's just as likely that Afanti was just cleaning the dressing room that they share with Cheeky Charlie and didn't want to say that because it didn't sound suitably spiritual.

Dora Affenberk has the exact same motive as Afanti and seemed to have some kind of connection to Gottle, apparently knowing him from school, but not 'that kind' of school. So, what kind? She was seen eavesdropping on audience members and Cook mentioned that it was she who normally fed Afanti his 'predictions', so it seems likely she was the one who told him to predict a death.

Then Radford remembered that Gottle had had a ventriloquism school, one he'd wanted to attend himself. Now suddenly the significance of Dora being in front of Gottle's door when he was heard inside became clear. It also explained why an overhearing Miss Dill felt his Bs had improved, when Cheeky Charlie's impersonation of Gottle had made it clear that he couldn't pronounce the Bs in 'Bing Crosby' or 'battle of the baritones'. It wasn't Gottle's voice that Miss Dill and others heard, it was Dora's. She was using her ventriloquist skills to make it seem as if he was inside, talking, when in fact he was already dead, stabbed in the stomach by her with a kitchen knife.

The other detail that had made him realise this was the blonde hairs Axton picked off the dummy when he got it out of the urn. Miss Dill had bright red hair, but Dora had a 'golden pile' of hair. Cook had said that Gottle once treated Malcolm like a weapon so had he used the dummy to try to defend himself against Dora?

Under interrogation Dora cracked. She insisted her husband had no idea, that Gottle had thrown her out of the ventriloquism school years ago because she was better than him and seeing her again seemed to think she wouldn't bear a grudge and would be interested in him. So, she met him in his room and attacked him, knowing her husband's noisy vacuuming in the nearby room would cover the sound. Then she threw her voice outside the room to make it seems as if they both had alibis for the murder, before feeding her husband the death prediction as a way of hopefully turning her desperate act into something that might benefit his career.

49. Happy Families

Helen Parnacki suspects that Jolyon Tenscott shot Geraint O'Mordha. And she suspects that Geraint O'Mordha himself was the spy.

Helen knew the plan was an ineffective way of trying to work out who was guilty. Anyone who had been a spy for that long would not be taken in by such an obvious ruse. And Geraint was no fool, so why would he decide on this plan in the first place?

And why would one of the suspects shoot him anyway? He was merely in the act of supposedly offering up classified knowledge. Even if they thought they had been exposed it would be simpler to not rise to the bait and return home.

For a wild second she had thought Mr Twill might have shot him thinking from his comments that Geraint was an embezzler, but Twill's chosen method of justice was the audit, not the gun.

The gun used didn't seem to be visible and none of the people seemed to be armed.

When the light had gone out, she had heard a hissing noise, then the gunshot and then movement, so whoever fired the shot must have done it from where they were. She found out later the hissing noise was caused by turning a knob in the desk drawer so it must have been Geraint who did it, and the desk drawer also has a switch which may, like the switch behind the lamp, enabled him to turn off the lights. She then remembered her observation of Geraint's love of dramatic espionage elements like 'rooms filled with poisonous gas', and how the room's door was reinforced and designed to be sealed. Helen surmised that the desk was equipped to send poisonous gas into the room, with the door providing protection from it when closed. Then one of the room's occupants may have realised what he was doing and shot him, getting up and turning off the gas.

That person was clearly Jolyon Tenscott. He was in the room when the lights came back on, and Twill did remark on how quickly he could move. How did he shoot Geraint? Tenscott had made remarks about Mrs Croom's cane, and Helen remembered how determined Mrs Croom was that pistols could be hidden in objects. Furthermore, her cane was upside down when the lights came on and she was gripping it much more tightly afterwards. Tenscott could have grabbed the cane, shot Geraint and returned it quickly to Mrs Croom before he ran to turn off the gas.

And why did he know about the gas and how to recognise a hidden gun? Because Tenscott was an agent like Helen Parnacki, the 'loudest, most blustering man you could imagine' that Geraint had mentioned in the past. He had to eliminate Tenscott because he either suspected or knew that Geraint really was the mole in the department.

Helen was able to confirm this with Tenscott privately. Geraint apparently had told him that they were there to trap Helen, and Tenscott said he thought it likely Geraint intended to kill all three of them with the gas and blame Helen for it, fleeing the country. Tenscott said he was probably going to inherit Geraint's position so it all worked out for the best as he was sick of having to run around everywhere and would like a desk job.

Helen assured Tenscott that she was not tired of running around, uncovering spies and investigating... curious cases.

50. Gwendolyn

Detective Inspector Radford suspects that Mark Swan robbed the safe. But he suspects that Katharine Piper killed her husband Oswald.

Regarding the theft, it was known that Oswald was very dedicated to Katharine so she had no need to steal any money as she would inherit it from him. Catcher knew about the safe and had apparently figured out the combination, and also the doll and the gun were found underneath his bed. However, he was famously squeamish and therefore unlikely to be able to shoot Piper without passing out. He could have been lying about this, but other checks would be able to prove if his claim was true or not. Furthermore, he seemed to genuinely care for Oswald and claimed he did think there was any money in the safe.

Mark Swan has big debts, and he was aware that Oswald had more money than him, saying he was generous. It was also known Oswald was taken to boasting about his safe. The manner in which he ended up staying at the Piper's house could be easily engineered by pretending to be drunk. Furthermore, Oswald was apparently also rather obvious about his safe code, 1812. Perhaps this indicates what Catcher said is true, and that there was no money in there at all, but rather only Gwendolyn the doll.

It is only Katharine who deliberately claimed a particular amount of money in the safe. When asked about it she initially claimed it came from a bank but quickly backpedalled, perhaps because she realised that bank withdrawals could be checked.

The key to it all is Gwendolyn the doll. Katharine seems obsessed with it, and largely disregarding anything other than her doll, constantly pestering Radford about it. She said that it has no real value beyond her emotional attachment. So what if it was the only thing in the safe? How could she guarantee the police would properly search for something that to most people was worthless? Maybe if there was money missing too... and a murder to investigate! And so her husband, who said he would do anything for her, had to die.

After interrogating everyone Radford constructed the truth: Mark Swan pretended to be drunk and once everyone in the house was asleep, he sneaked down and opened the safe... only to find a doll, and not the money he was expecting. He smashed a window to make it look like a burglary, then impulsively grabbed the doll and ran upstairs, angry and frustrated. But Oswald and his wife were woken by the noise and came down to find the safe open and Gwendolyn gone. Katharine said Oswald seemed insufficiently unconcerned about the doll and seemed to care more about the safe. So, knowing about Catcher's brother's gun, she retrieved it and shot Oswald to spur on any police investigation. Swan claimed he intended to put the doll back when he heard the shot. Knowing he had not shot Oswald he suspected Katherine or Catcher but didn't want to expose his own crime. In the meantime, Katharine hid the gun under the bed, and then ironically Swan hid the doll under there to frame Catcher, not realising he had put it right next to the murder weapon...

51. The Golden Empress
Mary suspects Jack Tavernier is the criminal mastermind, the signalling method is music, and the crime will happen at Midnight.

Or should we say, MIDNITE. When Mary became aware there might be a boat following the ship, she realised it would be a good method of getting the gold off the Empress without people realising. But the boat would need to know when it was going to happen. She briefly suspected that maybe Van Bruegel's group were using coloured scarves to signal to the boat, or perhaps Sir Rodney's groups hats had some significance. But the boat would be too far away in the mist to see those.

The ship's radio communications were being monitored by Dobson and his men. But there was one broadcast they weren't monitoring, exactly: The BBC's broadcast of the band's performance! A coded message could be sent that way. At first she wondered if the different keys of the songs was the way the message was being sent, but once she wrote the song titles down, she realised the clue was in their names: their initials!

Makin' Whoopee (G)

It Had To Be You (E major)

Dinah (C sharp)

Nobody Knows You When You're Down And out (A minor)

I Ain't Got Nobody (B flat)

Toot Toot Tootsie (C7)

Empty Bed Blues (F)

MIDNITE. The following ship would hear the BBC live broadcast and know when it was time. And the last song would just be her and Tavernier on stage, allowing the rest of the band to do the heist!

Thinking quickly, she grabbed the microphone and instead launched into a bravura performance of Stardust by Hoagie Carmichael! She hoped the boat would be confused enough by MIDNITS to pause in their attempt. And the band couldn't leave the stage! Until Dobson had them all arrested, that is. As they were marched off, Dobson remarked to her "This Jazz... It's quite jolly stuff really, Miss!"